W9-CTA-689

WWEST's
Gender Diversity in STEM

A briefing on women in science and engineering

Rebekah Parker   Jennifer Pelletier   Elizabeth Croft

The University of British Columbia

WWEST's Gender Diversity in STEM: A briefing on women in science and engineering.

© 2015 Rebekah Parker, Jennifer Pelletier, & Elizabeth Croft

Free digital copies of the Gender Diversity 101 papers can be found online at:
wwest.mech.ubc.ca/diversity

Printed in the United States of America

First Printing, 2015

Excerpt from "Evidence that gendered wording in job advertisement exists and sustains gender inequality" by D. Gaucher, J. Friesen, & A. Kay © 2011 Journal of Personality and Social Psychology. Reprinted with the permission of authors.

Published by Blurb
San Francisco, CA

Ordering Information:
Additional copies may be purchased online through the Blurb store.

Text layout & cover design by Rebekah Parker & Jennifer Pelletier
Cover photo by Jennifer Pelletier

Contents

Foreword

Dr. Elizabeth Croft, P.Eng., FEC, FASME
NSERC Chair for Women in Science and Engineering, BC/Yukon, 2010-2015
Associate Dean, Education and Professional Development, UBC Faculty of Applied Science
Professor, UBC Department of Mechanical Engineering | Director, CARIS Laboratory at UBC

The problem of under-representation of women in STEM (Science, Technology, Engineering and Math) has been widely discussed and written about in the literature. Significant efforts around the globe are underway to address this very important issue which, after all, involves 50% of the population. As an academic, a researcher, and an engineer, my preference has always been for explanations based on data sets rather than anecdotal experience. Engineering problem solving is grounded in collecting and evaluating data.

That said, when considering this problem, the individual stories — small comments by a peer, a parent or a teacher – "why do you want to take physics?", "Engineering?! Why would you want to do that?" or "I don't know…. honours math is really hard – are you sure?" — form a sort of collective dataset that reveals how doubt and insecurity creep in at a pivotal time in a young person's experience. Similarly, in the early career phase, experiences such as the unspoken assumption that "she" is the secretary and "he" is the engineer add up, eroding self-confidence even further. These micro-barriers can grow into walls plastered with big, unfriendly "do not enter" signs. I had been mostly oblivious to these barriers until one day a graduate advisor called me in to his office and explained to me —after telling me I was bright and had potential – that an academic career would be incompatible with having children. I was too stunned to ask him if that advice applied to him, his (at the time nearly 100% male) colleagues, and the male graduate students in the department. My confidence took a serious hit, and I began to question myself. Do I belong? Can I do this? Why am I swimming upstream? Maybe this isn't the right thing for me, I thought. Obviously, I carried on despite his advice.

I frequently share the stories of my experience as a student, an engineer, and an academic. I point out the uncomfortable questions I had. Where were all the girls in physics 12? Where were the women's washrooms in the machine shop facility? My hope is that our collective, anecdotal dataset will serve to help others see the barriers, know that they can be overcome, and ultimately, eliminated.

I've been very fortunate to have had family, friends and colleagues, male and female, who have encouraged me to pursue this path. They have supported, sponsored and mentored me. I have had peers who have lived the women in engineering adventure with me, and that shared experience has been greatly validating. A number of colleagues have very graciously contributed to this work – and I hope their stories, comments and anecdotes will strike a chord with the readers of this book.

The research described in this book helps explain the why behind the experiences. The white papers explore issues like the double bind that many women experience in their careers, the impact of stereotype threat, the effects of implicit bias and gendered language, and the ways in which men and women are viewed differently and respond differently to societal beliefs and norms. By understanding our own implicit bias we can get past those 'first seven seconds,' take a second look and see the underlying potential of the person in front of us. (Note: I did the Harvard Implicit Bias test and yes, I associate Male with Science and Engineering and Female with Humanities and Social Science.)

Together with Jennifer Pelletier and Rebekah Parker, I hope that this collection will help explain both why women do not choose certain careers in as large numbers as men and how we can, together, work to make change in our decisions, words, and actions to get to a world where participation in STEM is truly representative across all groups. As articulated in our white paper on the business case, it just makes economic sense. From an even broader perspective, we need the best, brightest and most diverse group of people contributing to Science and Engineering solutions to address some of the most challenging and urgent problems on the planet.

This book will be successful if it leads to action. There are things you can do to make change, right now, as a leader in your workplace, school, industry and community:

- Be aware that you have implicit biases and try to uncover them.
- Be inclusive – in your words, in your presentations and marketing materials, in your teams and networks.
- Support and implement people-friendly policies. Provide access to childcare and flexibility for managing family and other responsibilities. Schedule key meetings during core hours to allow maximum participation, and choose team-building activities that make everyone feel welcome.

My heartfelt thanks go out to the many people who have contributed to this work by writing the commentaries, reviewing the literature, proofreading the white papers and test-marketing the messaging. Like every good engineering project, this has been a team effort.

Read, share, act!

- Elizabeth

Acknowledgements

Thank you to the early readers of the Gender Diversity 101 white papers for your feedback and encouragement.

Thank you to the organizations who co-branded our Gender Diversity 101 white papers and continue to spread this message beyond WWEST 2010-2015.

We would also like to acknowledge the sponsors of the 2010-2015 NSERC Chair for Women in Science and Engineering for BC and Yukon. Without their support, WWEST would not be possible:

Natural Sciences and Engineering Research Council of Canada
The University of British Columbia, Faculty of Applied Science
BC Hydro
WorleyParsons
Teck
Stantec
Dr. Ken Spencer
Henry F. Man
Ms. Catherine Roome
Mr. Stanley Cowdell
Division for the Advancement of Women in Engineering and Geoscience
Nemetz (S/A) & Associates Ltd.
Glotman Simpson Consulting Engineers
Karen Savage, P.Eng.
Golder Associates Ltd.

How to Use This Book

This book is part research trends, part perspective. It is divided into twelve sections, each with an illustrated summary of the latest research on the topic, followed by a perspective from an expert in that area, or a member of the science, technology, engineering, and mathematics (STEM) academic and industry communities.

Unless noted, the authors of this content are Rebekah Parker, Jennifer Pelletier, and Elizabeth Croft. Copies of the infographic papers can be found online for free at wwest.mech.ubc.ca/diversity .

The research cited in the following pages reflect trends and may not capture the experience of all STEM workers, and community members. It does, however, reflect broader trends that are important to acknowledge and consider as we work to make STEM environments – whether in academia, industry, or communities – more inclusive and supportive of all identities.

While some research in this book compares women's experience to men's, we recognize that gender goes beyond the male/female binary. Experiences of people who identify as trans*, genderqueer, or gender variant identities may not be captured in the current research. For more information about creating trans* and gender variant inclusive workplaces visit: http://www.ohrc.on.ca/en/gender-identity-and-gender-expression-brochure/

As STEM fields become more diverse, we must ensure that we are not focused on gender as the sole metric indicating diversity, and recognize that barriers to STEM education and employment are not experienced in the same way for all people. Many of the topics in this book, like unconscious bias, microaggressions, and social identity threat, affect people beyond their gender identities.

At their core, the suggestions in this book are good people policies. Taking action on these should not be done in the name of improving conditions for one group, rather to enhance our communities and workplaces as spaces that accept and support the many identities that exist in STEM fields.

This book is a call to action: share the information in these pages with decision-makers and colleagues. Continue to call on our STEM communities to examine their policies, practices, and behaviours, and actively find ways to make your communities more inclusive for all. Continue the demand for more research on these topics, and stay up to date with the latest findings. Most of all, model change in your communities.

This is a starting place for much needed conversations; it is up to you and all STEM community members to continue them, and take action.

On Microaggressions

A quick glance, side comment, or gesture may seem harmless at first. However, dozens of glances quickly add up - over days, weeks, months, years - and send a message to the recipient: you are different; you do not belong. While in many cases these microaggressions are unintentional, the overall effect is damaging. The first step in reducing this harm is recognizing and acknowledging our subtle actions that can send inappropriate messages to members of our community. We may not realize the full impact of our (unconscious) actions until someone draws our attention to it. Microaggressions are a developing field in social science research, and a critical aspect of educating workplaces and communities about creating spaces that are safe and inclusive for all.

Microaggressions

Microaggressions are subtle, mundane exchanges that communicate hostile, derogatory, or negative messages to individuals based on group membership.[1,2] They can be verbal, behavioural, or environmental,[1] and include staring, glaring, comments, actions, and gestures.

These actions are not always conscious, yet are constant - often daily - experiences for people of colour, women, LGBTQ+ communities, people with disabilities, and members of other under-represented groups.[24]

Why Does This Matter for STEM Professions?

Microaggressions are prevalent across social environments; they exist in media coverage[25], clinical therapy[26], classrooms[21], academia[3], workplaces[27], and communities[19]. They are powerful because of the subtle, negative messages they often send[1], including that the person does not belong, and they deviate from the accepted norms. These messages are often unconscious and unintentional.

In order to address the lack of diversity in STEM fields, individuals and organizations must acknowledge their unconscious biases and behaviours. Microaggressions are interpersonal and institutional[28]; they can be as simple as unintentionally excluding a person from an important conversation[27].

Education and reflection - individually, communally, and institutionally - are critical steps to making workplace and community environments inclusive to all people, regardless of the groups they identify with. Once identified, action is needed to correct policies and behaviours that have the potential to harm and discriminate against members of our communities.

Prevalence & Effects

College students of colour experienced an average of **291 microaggressions** over 90 days.[3]

Microaggressions:

Negatively impact **mental health**.[4-9]	Decrease **productivity** & **problem-solving** abilities.[10,12,13]
Perpetuate **stereotype threat**.[10,11]	Create **hostile** work & institutional **environments**.[14,15]

What Can We Do?

To address microaggressions, learn to:[2,22]

Define them
especially "invisible" ones

Recognize them
In ourselves, and others

Deconstruct their hidden meanings

Acknowledge their effects
& learn about coping strategies

Take action[23,25]
Implement education programs

Types of Microaggressions[2]

Microassaults[2]
(often conscious)

Aims to **attack the a person's group identity**, or harm them through **name-calling**, **avoidance**, and **discriminatory actions**.[16,17]

Occurs when the perpetrator:[18]

has a level of anonymity	is among like-minded people	loses control

Microinsults[2]
(often unconscious)

Conveys a **stereotype**, **rudeness**, or **insensitivity** towards a person's group identity.

You are so well spoken for an immigrant!

Includes assumptions about the individual's:[2]

sexuality[19,20]   citizenship[1]
language abilities[21]   belonging[1]
intelligence[1]   gender[22]   criminality[1]

Microinvalidations[2]
(often unconscious)

Sexism doesn't exist.

Denies, excludes, & negates the **experiences** and **feelings** of an individual in a group.

May lead individuals to **question their experience**. Their response to the negative interaction may be **perceived as a irrational overreaction.**[2]

References

1. Sue, D.W., Capodilupo, C. M., Torino, G. C., Bucceri, J. M., Holder, A. M. B., Nadal, K. L., & Esquilin,M. (2007). Racial microaggressions in everyday life: Implications for clinical practice. *American Psychologist, 62*, 271-286.

2. Sue, D.W. (2010). *Microaggressions in everyday life: Race, gender, and sexual orientation.* Hoboken, NJ: John Wiley & Sons.

3. Blume, A.W., Lovato, L.V., Thyken, B.N., & Denny, N. (2012). The relationship of microaggressions with alcohol use and anxiety among ethnic minority college students in a historically White institution. *Cultural Diversity & Ethnic Minority Psychology, 18*(1), 45-54.

4. Brondolo, E., Brady, N., Thompson, S., Tobin, J. N., Cassells, A., Sweeney, M., et al. (2008). Perceived racism and negative affect: Analysis of trait and state measures of affect in a community sample. *Journal of Social and Clinical Psychology, 27*, 150 – 173.

5. Crocker, J., & Major, B. (1989). Social stigma and self-esteem: The self-protective properties of stigma. *Psychological Review, 96*, 608 – 630.

6. Sue, D. W., Capodilupo, C. M., & Holder, A. (2008). Racial microaggressions in the life experience of Black Americans. *Professional Psychology: Research and Practice, 39*, 329– 336.

7. Swim, J. K., Hyers, L. L., Cohen, L. L., & Ferguson, M. J. (2001). Everyday sexism: Evidence for its incidence, nature, and psychological impact from three daily diary studies. *Journal of Social Issues, 57*, 31–53.

8. Huynh, V. W. (2012). Ethnic microaggressions and the depressive and somatic symptoms of Latino and Asian American adolescents. *Journal of Youth and Adolescence, 41*(7), 831-846.

9. Szymanski, D. M., & Gupta, A. (2009). Examining the relationship between multiple internalized oppressions and African American lesbian, gay, bisexual, and questioning persons' self-esteem and psychological distress. *Journal of Counseling Psychology, 56*(1), 110–118.

10. Cadinu, M., Maass, A., Rosabianca, A., & Kiesner, J. (2005). Why do women underperform under stereotype threat? Evidence for the role of negative thinking. *Psychological Science, 16*, 572 – 578.

11. Steele, C. M., Spencer, S. J., & Aronson, J. (2002). Contending with group image: The psychology of stereotype and social identity threat. In M. Zanna (Ed.), *Advances in Experimental Social Psychology* (Vol. 23, pp. 379 – 440). New York: Academic Press.

12. Dovidio, J. F. (2001). On the nature of contemporary prejudice: The third wave. *Journal of Social Issues, 57*, 829 – 849.

13. Salvatore, J., & Shelton, J. N. (2007). Cognitive costs of exposure to racial prejudice. *Psychological Science, 18*, 810 – 815.

14. Rowe, M. P. (1990). Barriers to equality: The power of subtle discrimination to maintain unequal opportunity. *Employee Responsibilities and Rights Journal, 3*, 153 – 163.

15. Solórzano, D., Ceja, M., & Yosso, T. (2000). Critical race theory, racial microaggressions, and campus racial climate: The experiences of African American college students. *The Journal of Negro Education, 69*(1/2) , 60 – 73.

16. Miller, J., & Garran, A. M. (2008). *Racism in the United States.* Belmont, CA: Brooks Cole.

17. Nelson, T. D. (2006). *The psychology of prejudice.* Boston: Pearson Publishers.

18. Sue, D. W., & Capodilupo, C. M. (2008). Racial, gender, and sexual orientation microaggressions: Implications for counseling and psychotherapy. In D. W. Sue & D. Sue (Eds.), *Counseling the culturally diverse: Theory and practice.* Hoboken, NJ: John Wiley & Sons.

19. Nadal, K.L., Issa, M-A., Leon, J., Meterko, V., Wideman, M., & Wong, Y. (2011). Sexual orientation microaggressions: "Death by a thousand cuts" for lesbian, gay, and bisexual youth. *Journal of LGBT Youth, 8*, 234-259.

20. Christman, S.T. (2012). Coping with homonegative experiences among gay men: Impacts on mental health, psychological well-being, and identity growth (Doctoral dissertation). Open Access Dissertations (Paper 775).

21. López Levia, C.A., & Khisty, L.L. (2014). "Juntos pero no revueltos": Microaggressions and language in mathematics education of non-dominant Latina/os. *Mathematics Education Resource Journal, 2*, 421-438.

22. Ross-Sheriff, F. (2012). Microaggression, women and social work. *Affilia: Journal of Women and Social Work, 27*(3), 233-236.

23. Offermann, L.R., Basford, T.E., Graebner, R., DeGraaf, S.B., & Jaffer, S. (2013). Slights, snubs, and slurs: Leader equity and microaggressions. *Equality, Diversity and Inclusion: An International Journal, 32*(4), 374-393.

24. Nadal, K.L., Davidoff, K.C., Davis, L.S., Wong, Y., Marshall, D., & McKenzie, V. (2015). A qualitative approach to intersectional microaggressions: Understanding influences of race, ethnicity, gender, sexuality and religion. *Qualitative Psychology, 2*(2), 147-163.

25. Kaskan, E.R., & Ho, I.K. (2014). Microaggressions and female athletes. *Sex Roles.* Retrieved from http://link.springer.com/article/10.1007%2Fs11199-014-0425-1#/

26. Shelton, K., & Delgado-Romero, E.A. (2011). Sexual orientation microaggressions: The experience of lesbian, gay, bisexual, and queer clients in psychotherapy. *Journal of Counselling Psychology, 58*(2), 210-221.

27. Basford, T.E., Offermann, L.R., & Behrand, T.S. (2014). Do you see what I see? Perceptions of gender microaggressions in the workplace. *Psychology of Women Quarterly, 38*(3), 340-349.

28. Yosso, T.J., Smith, W.A., Ceja, M., & Solorzano, D.G. (2009). Critical race theory, racial microaggressions, and campus racial climate for Latina/o undergraduates. *Harvard Educational Review, 79*(4), 659-690.

Recommended Readings

1. Robinson, J.L. (2014). Sexual orientation microaggressions and posttraumatic stress symptoms. (Doctoral dissertation, Texas Women's University).

2. Sue, D.W. (2010). *Microaggressions in everyday life: Race, gender, and sexual orientation.* Hoboken, NJ: John Wiley & Sons.

3. Zesiger, H. (2013). *Racial microaggressions and college student wellbeing: An annotated bibliography for student affairs and health promotion professionals in higher education.* Office of Health Promotion, Emory University. Retrieved from http://studenthealth.emory.edu/hp/documents/pdfs/Racial%20Microaggressions%20and%20College%20Student%20Wellbeing.pdf

Perspective References

1. Judson, S.S. (2014). *Sexist discrimination and gender microaggressions: An exploration of current conceptualizations of women's experiences of sexism.* (Doctoral dissertation, The University of Akron). Retrieved from OhioLINK Electronic Theses & Dissertations Center. (akron1404865988).

2. Owen, J., Tao, K., & Rodolfa, E. (2010). Microaggressions and women in short-term psychotherapy: Initial evidence. *The Counselling Psychology, 38*(7), 923-946.

3. Camacho, M.M., & Lord, S.M. (2011). Microaggressions in engineering education: Climate for Asian, Latina and White women. In *Frontiers in Education Conference (FIE)*, 2011 (pp. S3H-1). IEEE.

4. Nadal, K.L., Issa, M-A., Leon, J., Meterko, V., Wideman, M., & Wong, Y. (2011). Sexual orientation microaggressions: "Death by a thousand cuts" for lesbian, gay, and bisexual youth. *Journal of LGBT Youth, 8*, 234-259.

Gender and Microaggressions

Ms. Sarah Moroz, M.Sc.
Ph.D. Candidate, University of Western Ontario Department of Psychology

"Why are we talking about this? Women don't really face any discrimination these days anyway."

A male friend of mine once said this to me after I had made a comment about the challenges faced by women in the workplace. Several years later, I still remember the dismay I felt at that statement. Surely my friend couldn't believe that sexism was over.

Sexism is, of course, alive and kicking. And perhaps ironically, the denial of sexism has been identified as a form of discrimination itself. It falls under the category of microaggressions: subtle, often-unconscious messages of negativity or hostility directed toward members of marginalized groups.

Denial of sexism is just one of many different kinds of microaggressions. Past research has identified various other categories of gender-based microaggressions, including objectification, appearance pressure, traditional household duty expectations, marriage and child-bearing expectations, harshly labeled assertiveness, and patriarchal work expectations.[1] Importantly, the same study also suggested that microaggressions were a distinct form of discrimination; that is, microaggressions didn't overlap enough with more classical forms of sexism to be considered redundant.

But why does any of this matter? Microaggressions are often so subtle and difficult to interpret that, to outsiders, they may seem completely harmless. However, microaggressions aren't usually experienced in isolation; they're often characterized as constant, continuing experiences, and the weight of these combined experiences can be greater than the sum of their parts. In fact, scholarly work has shown that microaggressions can have negative consequences on their targets. For instance, experiences of microaggressions have been linked to greater levels of psychological distress.[1] Women who report a greater incidence of microaggressions from their therapists tend to display a deceased working alliance and more negative therapy outcomes.[2] Other work has shown that female students in male-dominated fields, such as engineering, report feelings of isolation, stress, and invalidation as a result of gender-based microaggressions.[3]

We can also draw from work conducted on microaggressions in other fields. The academic study of microaggressions first began in the field of racial relations, and has only more recently been applied to marginalized groups based on gender, sexual orientation, and disability. These other forms of microaggressions have been linked with lower self-esteem, post-traumatic symptoms, lower feelings of subjective well-being and value, physical health problems like headaches and poor appetite, and even shorter life expectancies.[4]

Gender-based microaggressions are still understudied and not yet fully understood, but the scientific community is making progress in exploring this subtle form of discrimination. If nothing else, it's clear by now that the concept of microaggressions is useful in understanding the marginalization of women and the consequences thereof.

So to answer my friend: that's why we're talking about this.

On the Business Case

Striving for diversity in your organization says a lot about your values, but it also makes good business sense. Diverse teams are more innovative. Employees in diverse organizations are more satisfied at work. Diverse organizations outperform their competitors.

Increasing diversity in your organization is an investment in your future performance.

COSTCO WHOLESALE

WAREHOUSE #256

799 McCallum Road
LANGFORD BC V9B-6A2
MEMBER #111753502536 K6

295701 KS ND TURKEY	43.99	
512615 STRAWBERRIES	12.99	
222886 ALWYS LNR200	14.49	
1049391 TPD/222886	3.00-	
16155A KS DUE PASA	5.79	
162200 MINI BABYBEL	10.99	
1049363 TPD/162200	2.40-	
188041 PICO SALSA	8.49	
5086 CHEESTRINGS	12.89	
954600 RICE PUDDING	8.49	
1782 CHOC MILK 4L	5.59	
430 X-LARGE EGGS	6.89	
347937 ROTI CHICKEN	7.99	
1666 SANDWICH WM	6.29	
1050781 TPD/DEMPSTER	2.00-	

SUBTOTAL	137.48	
**** (G)GST 5%	2.89	
**** (P)PST 7%	3.08	
TOTAL	143.45	
VF MasterCard	143.45	

```
xxxxxxxxxxxx5597
REFERENCE#: 662307245-001001B130
AUTH#: 035395           02/25/16 14:51
Invoice#: 37161
```

COSTCO # 256
799 McCallum Road
Langford, BC V9B-6A2

PURCHASE - MASTERCARD
Mastercard
A0000000041010
0000008000 E800
01 APPROVED - THANK YOU 027
AMOUNT: $143.45

0256 008 000000097 0172

IMPORTANT - retain this copy for your
record.

*** CARDHOLDER COPY ***

CHANGE	.00	
TOTAL DISCOUNT(S)	7.40	

TOTAL NUMBER OF ITEMS SOLD = 12
CASHIER: Daniel M.   REG# 8
02/25/2016 14:51 0256 08 0172 37

GST #121475329
THANK YOU, PLEASE COME AGAIN!

WAREHOUSE #256

799 McCallum Road
LANGFORD BC V9B-6A2
MEMBER #111753502536 K6

```
 295701 KS ND TURKEY     43.99 
 512515 STRAWBERRIES     12.99
 222886 ALWYS LNR200     14.49
1046991 TPD/222886        3.00-
 161552 KS QUE PASA       5.79 
 162200 MINI BABYBEL     10.99
1049953 TPD/162200        2.40-
 188041 PICO SALSA        8.49
   5086 CHEESTRINGS      12.89
 964600 RICE PUDDING      8.49
   1782 CHOC MILK 4L      5.59
    430 X-LARGE EGGS      6.89
 347937 ROTI CHICKEN      7.99 
   1666 SANDWICH WHT      6.29
1050781 TPD/DEMPSTER      2.00-

        SUBTOTAL        137.48
  **** (G)GST 5%          2.89
  **** (P)PST 7%          3.08

        TOTAL           143.45
VF      MasterCard      143.45
```

```
***********5597
REFERENCE#: 66230739-0010018130
AUTH#: 03539S        02/25/16 14:51:
Invoice#: 31761

COSTCO # 256
799 McCallum Road
Langford. BC  V9B-6A2

PURCHASE - MASTERCARD
MasterCard
A0000000041010
0000008000 E800
    01 APPROVED - THANK YOU 027
       AMOUNT: $143.45

    0256 008 0000000097 0172
```

IMPORTANT - retain this copy for you
record.

*** CARDHOLDER COPY ***

```
    CHANGE                   .00
    TOTAL DISCOUNT(S)       7.40

TOTAL NUMBER OF ITEMS SOLD =  12
CASHIER: Daniel M.          REG# 8
2016/02/25 14:51 0256 08 0172 97
```

GST #121476329
THANK YOU, PLEASE COME AGAIN!

The Business Case for Gender Diversity

Over 20 years of research demonstrates a correlation between organizations with high gender diversity in leadership and several measures of organizational success.

Gender diversity is linked to employee satisfaction,[1] improved governance and innovation. It is also associated with financial benefits, including a positive impact on firm value.[2]

While some boards do currently have female members, discrimination still exists as women are more likely to be board members than chairs.[23]

To benefit from gender diversity, organizations should avoid tokenism and ensure there is a "critical mass" of women represented.[17,21,22] This means having at least 2-3 women, or at least 30% of the board.

While correlation does not indicate causation, there is a clear relationship between an organization's gender diversity and aspects of their success. Longitudinal studies found a correlation between promoting women to executive positions and high profitability over 20+ years.[8]

In order for change to occur, a paradigm shift is needed where organizations' leadership values diversity, recognizes the challenge of expressing diverse opinions, and aims to support the professional development of all employees.[18]

More Innovation

If a group includes more women, the collective intelligence rises[19]

Gender diversity has a positive effect on team innovation in radical research[20]

Having a critical mass of 30% or at least 2 or 3 women on a board decreases **groupthink**[21]

Access to More Talent

2006 Canadian Census[16]

♀ **47.4**% of workforce

♀ **21.9**% of engineering & science workforce

Diverse hiring increases the recruiting pool[17] and is a more effective use of talent and leadership[18]

Improved Governance

Gender diverse boards are more likely to allocate effort into corporate monitoring, and increase participation in decision-making.[10]

Women directors:

improve a firm's ability to navigate complex strategic issues[12]

positively influence board strategic direction & tasks[11,14]

women are more "prepared to push the 'tough issues'"[13]

reduce conflict on boards[14] & negative corporate social practices[15,24]

Economic Benefits

Fortune 500 companies with the most women on board of directors outperformed companies with the least.[4,5,6,7,8]

Similar results apply to Canadian corporations.[9]

- Bottom Quartile WBD
- Top Quartile WBD

+16% 13.4% / 11.6% — Return on Sales[4]

+26% 9.1% / 7.2% — Return on Invested Capital[4]

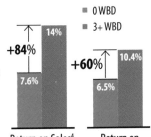

- 0 WBD
- 3+ WBD

+84% 14% / 7.6% — Return on Sales[4]

+60% 10.4% / 6.5% — Return on Invested Capital[4]

*WBD: Women Board Directors; stats from 2004-2008

References

1. Orser, B. (2000). *Creating high-performance organizations: Leveraging women's leadership.* Retrieved from the Conference Board of Canada website: http://www.conferenceboard.ca/

2. Campbell, K. & Mínguez-Vera, A. (2008). Gender diversity in the boardroom and firm financial performance. *Journal of Business Ethics, 83*(3), 435-451.

3. Grosvold, J. (2011). Where are all the women? Institutional context and the prevalence of women on the corporate board of directors. *Business & Society, 50*(3), 531– 555.

4. Catalyst (2011). *The bottom line: Corporate performance and women's representation on boards (2004–2008).* Retrieved from http://www.catalyst.org/knowledge/bottom-line-corporate-performance-and-womens-representation-boards-20042008

5. Catalyst (2004). *The bottom line: Connecting corporate performance and gender diversity.* Retrieved from http://www.catalyst.org/knowledge/bottom-line-connecting-corporate-performance-and-gender-diversity

6. Catalyst (2007). *The bottom line: Corporate performance and women's representation on boards.* Retrieved from http://www.catalyst.org/knowledge/bottom-line-corporate-performance-and-womens-representation-boards

7. Adler, R. D. (1999). *Women in the executive suite correlate to high profits.* Retrieved from the European Project on Equal Pay website: http://www.w2t.se/se/filer/adler_web.pdf

8. Adler, R. (2009, February 27). Profit, thy name is ... woman? *Pacific Standard: The Science of Society.* Retrieved from http://www.psmag.com/navigation/business-economics/profit-thy-name-is-woman-3920/

9. Brown, D. A. A., Brown, D.L. & Anastasopoulos, V. (2002). *Women on boards: Not just the right thing ... But the "bright" thing.* Retrieved from The Conference Board of Canada website: http://www.conferenceboard.ca/

10. Adams, R., & Ferreira, D. (2009). Women in the boardroom and their impact on governance and performance. *Journal of Financial Economics, 94*(2), 291–309.

11. Lückerath-Rovers, M. (2013). Women on boards and firm performance. *Journal of Management & Governance, 17*(2), 491-509.

12. Francoeur, C., Labelle, R., & Sinclair-Desgagné, B. (2008). Gender diversity in corporate governance and top management. *Journal of Business Ethics, 81*(1), 83-95.

13. Estlad, B., & Ladegard, G. (2012). Women on corporate boards: Key influences or tokens? *Journal of Management & Governance, 16*(4), 595-615.

14. Nielsen, S., & Huse, M. (2010). The contribution of women on boards of directors: Going beyond the surface. *Corporate Governance: An International Review, 18*(2), 136-148.

15. Boulouta, I. (2013). Hidden connections: The link between board gender diversity and corporate social performance. *Journal of Business Ethics, 113*(2), 185-197.

16. Statistics Canada. (2006). *Occupation - National Occupational Classification for Statistics 2006 (720), Class of Worker (6) and Sex (3) for the Labour Force 15 Years and Over of Canada, Provinces, Territories, Census Metropolitan Areas and Census Agglomerations, 2006 Census - 20% Sample Data.* (Catalogue number 97-559-XCB2006011). Retrieved from http://www12.statcan.gc.ca/

17. Mathisen, G. E., Ogaard, T., & Marnburg, E. (2013). Women in the boardroom: How do female directors of corporate boards perceive boardroom dynamics? *Journal of Business Ethics, 116*(1), 87–97.

18. Mannix, E., & Neale. M.A. (2005). What differences make a difference? The promise and reality of diverse teams in organizations. *Psychological Science in the Public Interest, 6*(2), 31-55.

19. Woolley, A., Malone, T. & Berinato, (2011). What makes a team smarter? More women. *Harvard Business Review, 89* (6), 32-33. Retrieved from http://hbr.org/2011/06/defend-your-research-what-makes-a-team-smarter-more-women/ar/1

20. Diaz-Garcia, C., Gonzalez-Moreno, A., & Saez-Martinez, F.J. (2013). Gender diversity within R&D teams: Its impact on radicalness of innovation. *Innovation: Management, Policy, & Practice, 15*(2), 149- 160.

21. Torchia, M., Calabrò, A., & Huse, M. (2011). Women directors on corporate boards: From tokenism to critical mass. *Journal of Business Ethics, 102*(2), 299–317.

22. Joecks, J., Kerstin, P., & Vetter, K. (2013). Gender diversity in the boardroom and firm performance: What exactly constitutes a "critical mass?" *Journal of Business Ethics, 118*(1), 61-72.

23. Simpson, G., Carter, D.A., & D'Souza, F. (2010). What do we know about women on boards? *Journal of Applied Finance, 20*(2), 27-39.

24. Galbreath, J. (2011). Are there gender-related influences on corporate sustainability? A study of women on boards of directors. *Journal of Management and Organization, 17*(1),17-38.

Recommended Readings

1. McCauley, C. (1989). The nature and social influence in groupthink: Compliance and internalization. *Journal of Personality and Social Psychology, 57*(2), 250-260.

2. Shore, L.M., Chung-Herrera, B.G., Dean, M.A., Ehrhart, K.H., Jung, D.I., Randel, A.E., & Signh, G. (2009). Diversity in organizations: Where are we now and where are we going? *Human Resource Management Review, 19*(2), 117-133.

3. Singh, V., & Vinnicombe, S. (2004). Why so few women directors in top UK boardrooms? Evidence and theoretical explanations. *Corporate Governance: An International Review,12*(4), 479-488.

Increasing Canada's Competitiveness

Ms. Maryse Belanger, P.Geo.
CEO and Managing Director, Mirabela Nickel Ltd.

The need for Canada to increase its competitiveness clearly underpins the business case for gender diversity in STEM. Competitiveness is defined by the World Economic Forum as the set of institutions, policies, and factors that determine the level of productivity of a country. The level of productivity, in turn, sets the level of prosperity that can be earned by an economy. In other words, a more competitive economy is one that is likely to sustain growth.

Canada's world ranking in competitiveness has been declining in recent years and stands now at fourteen. Consider some of the twelve main factors that drive overall competitiveness. Higher education and training, plus technological readiness, support increased efficiency of a country's economy. Business sophistication and innovation are the most critical factors that define competitiveness.

The recently published Global Gender Gap Reports (World Economic Forum) include data for approximately ninety-two percent of the global population. They show a strong correlation between gender inequality and a country's competitiveness, particularly a country's investment in its human talent and the opportunities created for women. Ensuring appropriate use of half of the world's available talent thus has a vast bearing on how competitive a country may become. At a smaller scale, utilizing the entire talent pool affects how efficient a company may be.

To maximize competitiveness, Canada ought to strive for gender diversity in all areas of its economy, which means that men and women have not only the same rights and responsibilities, but also the same opportunities.

In the business world, it has been demonstrated that gender diversity at all levels of an organization has a positive impact on financial performance. Companies that include more women at the top levels of leadership tend to outperform those that include fewer. With a growing female talent pool coming out of schools and universities, companies who fail to recruit and retain women undermine their long-term competitiveness. Companies must also ensure they provide a pathway to leadership positions. For those that do, the benefits of gender diversity are evident.

In a highly interconnected and rapidly changing world, Canada must adapt strategies and innovate in order to remain relevant and competitive, augmenting the need for the creativity fostered by gender diversity. Diversity is also critical to informed decision-making; it helps avoid "group think," which can lead to poor decisions and unmitigated technical and business risks.

In the current economic and social turmoil it is more important than ever to increase economic participation among women and to regard this as an opportunity for progress. The input, talent and creative passion from both men and women are required to design and implement the most innovative solutions and improve the future.

Ultimately, gender diversity is fundamental to whether and how Canada thrives.

On Unconscious Biases

As scientists, engineers, and humans, we like to think of ourselves as unbiased decision makers – analytical people that can judge and weigh a situation without prejudice. We have policies about being unbiased in hiring selections, promotions, and other professional contexts, and as a society we denounce discrimination. Removing deliberate bias, however, does not solve the problem – it is only a first step. Unconscious biases affect our decision making every day, and these microbarriers can have a significant impact. The first step in countering unconscious biases is to be aware of them.

Unconscious Bias

Unconscious bias refers to the assumptions and conclusions we jump to without thinking.[1]

An example might be assuming that an older person walking with a child is their grandparent. These biases do not indicate hostility towards certain groups; they reflect how the individual has been socialized.

Several studies demonstrate the impact unconscious bias can have on the hiring process, particularly for women.

These biases may not be intentional, but their impact is severe. The effects of unconscious bias will not be overcome by maintaining our current efforts to recruit and retain more women.[2]

To reduce unconscious bias in hiring, committees and individuals need to be educated about its existence and effects in academia and industry.

Online tools such as the Harvard Implicit Association Test can help identify an individual's unconscious biases. Sharing research and becoming aware of your organization's hiring tendencies can also help reduce unconscious discrimination.

To be seen as equally "**competent**" by reviewers, female researchers need to publish:

3 more articles in *Nature* or *Science* **OR** **20 more** articles in specialist journals

than male applicants when applying for a medical fellowship.[5]

"We would have to see her job talk"

"I would need to see evidence that she had gotten these grants and publications on her own"

Psychology professors reviewing identical CVs were **4x** more likely to write **cautionary comments** for female applicants.[4]

Try the Implicit Bias test: https://implicit.harvard.edu/

Reference letters for female medical faculty were **shorter**, more **vague**, and placed **less emphasis on research** than those for males.[6]

Percentage of letters that contained the phrase:

"**compassionate**" or "**relates well with patients/staff**" — 16% / 4%

"**accomplishment**" and "**achievement**" — 3% / 13%

"**successful**" — 3% / 7%

■ ♀   ■ ♂

The average letter length for women was **227** words, compared to **253** words for men.[6]

US science professors were asked to evaluate a CV for a **lab manager**:[2]

$30,238.10 $26,507.94

♂   ♀

The male candidate was offered a **higher salary**...

... more **mentorship**

... and was rated more "**competent**" and "**hireable**."

♂ CV   ♀ CV

The catch? Other than the names at the top, the CVs were **identical**.[2]

Women are **50%** more likely to advance in an orchestra audition if they **can't be seen**.[3]

References

1. Network Exchange. (2012). *Unconscious bias.* Retrieved from http://online.fliphtml5.com/hcxu/wfbe/#p=6
2. Moss-Racusin, C. et al. (2012). Science faculty's subtle gender biases favor male students. *Proceedings of the National Academy of Sciences of the United States of America, 109*(41), 16474-16479.
3. Goldin, C. & Rouse, C. (2000). Orchestrating impartiality: The impact of "blind" auditions on female musicians. *The American Economic Review, 90*(4), 715-741.
4. Steinpreis, R., Andres, K. & Ritzke, D. (1999). The impact of gender on the review of the curricula vitae of job applicants and tenure candidates: A national empirical study. *Sex Roles, 41*(7/8), 509-528.
5. Wennerås, C. & Wold, A. (1997). Nepotism and sexism in peer-review. *Nature, 387,* 341-343.
6. Trix, F. & Psenka, C. (2003). Exploring the color of glass: Letters of recommendation for female and male medical faculty. *Discourse & Society, 14*(2), 191-220.

Recommended Readings

1. Coorice, A. (2009). Unconscious bias in faculty and leadership recruitment: A literature review. *Association of American Medical Colleges Analysis in Brief, 9*(2).
2. Harvard Implicit Association Test: https://implicit.harvard.edu/
3. Bertrand, M. & Mullainathan, S. (2003). Are Emily and Greg more employable than Lakisha and Jamal? A field experiment on labor market discrimination. *The American Economic Review, 94*(4), 991-1013.
4. Fine, E. & Handelsman, J. (2006). *Reviewing applicants: Research on bias and assumptions.* Women in Science & Engineering Leadership Institute (WISELI) University of Wisconsin-Madison. Retrieved from http://wiseli.engr.wisc.edu/docs/BiasBrochure_3rdEd.pdf

More resources can be found at: http://wiseli.engr.wisc.edu/

Dare to Question Your Unconscious Bias

Dr. Marc Parlange, P.Eng.
Dean, UBC Faculty of Applied Science

Stereotypes — over-generalized, exaggerated characterizations of a particular group of people — are common in our culture. Don't we all want our bankers to be Swiss, our cooks to be Italian and our lovers to be French?

Unlike stereotypes, which we by and large recognize, bias operates automatically, below the level of conscious awareness, colouring our attitudes towards other people based on things like their age, gender, ethnicity, or appearance. These knee-jerk reactions affect our understanding, decision-making and behaviour in ways we may not even be aware of. Biases form over a lifetime of programming from family, school, the media, advertising, and peer interaction. We all have biases; we can't help it. It's not good or bad — it's just a fact. Studies have shown that even the most enlightened among us have unconscious biases, and they are often diametrically opposed to our rationally derived, explicitly declared beliefs.

Implicit gender-role bias, in particular, is extremely pervasive in our culture. From pink and blue toys to subtle comments by family and teachers, children encounter this bias very early on. Later, they risk running into it in the classroom, in co-ops, with prospective employers and then in the workplace. Both women and men can be discouraged from entering disciplines and professions that could otherwise have greatly benefited from their talent, ideas and perspective.

The good news is that if something can be programmed, it can be reprogrammed. Shedding light on bias can bring it out of the shadows of the subconscious and into a place where it can be challenged and changed.

I've spent thirty-some years in academia, where implicit bias continues to be a problem. Student populations should logically reflect society — 50% men and 50% women. Yet disciplines like engineering and nursing on most campuses are seriously unbalanced, creating an environment that can be intimidating, if not outright hostile, to the minority group. And because the roots lie upstream in the early programming of girls and boys, it's a vicious cycle that's very hard to break.

But I believe it can be done and that it is our responsibility to address the problem. If universities embrace the challenge of unpacking and reprogramming these biases, then they can be the beginning of a sea change that will be of huge benefit to society. Effective practical steps have been identified, from mentoring, to recruiting efforts, to providing programs for younger children and their teachers.

As I see it, the ultimate goal is for university students in disciplines such as engineering to experience a new "normal" — a balanced population that reflects and encourages a diversity of ideas and approaches. These students, both male and female, will take away with them the expectation of encountering and encouraging this inclusive environment in the professional world and in their own families. Within a generation or two, that normal could take hold more widely, and the unconscious bias that is now so pervasive could be seen clearly for what it is – just another silly, outdated stereotype.

On Stereotype Threat

Have you ever been flustered when someone comes over to watch you work on something? It can be something you are really good at, but as they stand there you become more aware of what you are doing, and start wondering what they are thinking. These thoughts distract you from the task at hand, and you make errors. Something similar can happen when people experience stereotype threat – the concern of being viewed though the lens of a stereotype. A white man walks into a math exam, and someone remarks, "Asians are so good at math." A woman is interviewing for an engineering job, and overhears the receptionist telling someone that they are going to try interviewing a woman this time , but they have never had luck with women hires in the past. Suddenly, these tests are not just about skill – individuals have to contend with the stereotype, and the negative performance impact of the increased stress and self-awareness. Talking about stereotype threat and its effects is the first step towards overcoming it.

Stereotype Threat

Stereotype Threat

refers to the concern with being viewed through the lens of a stereotype.[1]

Stereotype threat is caused by cues in the situation that remind people of negative stereotypes.[13,18]

Anxiety over confirming these stereotypes can **impair** an individual's ability to perform up to their full potential.[2]

Research has shown that stereotype threat negatively impacts: women's math performance[3] (compared to men's), White men's math performance[4] (compared to Asian men), men's social sensitivity[5] and spatial abilities[6] (compared to women's), White athletic performance[7] (compared to Black), and Black students' verbal problem-solving abilities[1] (compared to White students').

Stereotype threat may be a significant factor in undermining women's success and persistence in engineering.[13] This has important implications for STEM fields. A simple reminder of one's race or gender is enough to elicit stereotype threat.[18]

STEM fields should consider ways to create identity safe environments to help people overcome stereotype threat.

By actively **raising awareness** about stereotype threat, providing **role models**, and **encouraging self-affirmation** exercises, individuals' performances are more likely to match their potential.

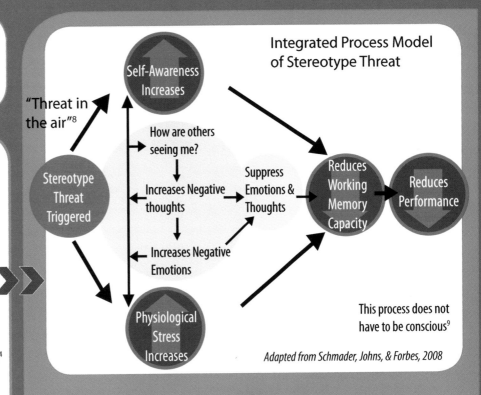

Integrated Process Model of Stereotype Threat

"Threat in the air"[8]

Stereotype Threat Triggered

Self-Awareness Increases

How are others seeing me?

Increases Negative thoughts

Increases Negative Emotions

Physiological Stress Increases

Suppress Emotions & Thoughts

Reduces Working Memory Capacity

Reduces Performance

This process does not have to be conscious[9]

Adapted from Schmader, Johns, & Forbes, 2008

Environment Triggers

Don't...

... define people by their gender,

You must be athletic!

... or their group,

"Women aren't good at math"

... or stereotype on performance expectations

Impact on STEM

Reduced:

Performance[18]

of women & minority students on the SAT, by 50 points[18]

Job Engagement & Organizational Commitment

in academia[11] & in the engineering industry[12]

Coping Strategies & Alleviating the Threat

Role Models
Show that others have struggled and succeeded [9,17,20]

Self-Affirmation
Write about your core values[21]

My Values

Reframe the Situation
Create identity safe contexts e.g. gender-fair tests[3]

Learn about Stereotype Threat
Performance improves when stereotype threat is explained before a test[14,15,19]

Stereotype Threat

Attribute the anxiety to the stereotype, not the self [14]

References

1. Steele, C.M., & Aronson, J. (1995). Stereotype threat and the intellectual test performance of African-Americans. *Journal of Personality and Social Psychology, 69,* 797-811.
2. Walton, G., & Spencer, S. (2009). Latent ability: Grades and test scores systematically underestimate the intellectual ability of negatively stereotyped students. *Psychological Science, 20*(9), 1132-1139.
3. Spencer, S.J., Steele, C.M., Quinn, D.M. (1999). Stereotype threat and women's math performance. *Journal of Experimental Social Psychology, 35*(1), 4-28.
4. Aronson, J., Lustina, M.J., Good, C., & Keough, K. (1999). When white men can't do math: Necessary and sufficient factors in stereotype threat. *Journal of Experimental Social Psychology, 35,* 29-46.
5. Leyens, J., Désert, M., Croizet, J., & Darcis, C. (2000). Stereotype threat: Are lower status and history of stigmatization preconditions of stereotype threat? *Personality and Social Psychology Bulletin, 26,* 1189-1199.
6. Wraga, M., Duncan, L., Jacobs, E., Helt, M., & Church, J. (2006). Stereotype susceptibility narrows the gender gap in imagined self-rotation performance. *Psychonomic Bulletin & Review. 13,* 813–819.
7. Stone, J., Lynch, C. I., Sjomeling, M., & Darley, J.M. (1999). Stereotype threat effects on black and white athletic performance. *Journal of Personality and Social Psychology, 77,* 1213–1227.
8. Steele, C.M. (1997). A threat in the air: How stereotypes shape intellectual identity and performance. *American Psychologist, 52*(6), 613–629.
9. Schmader, T., & Johns, M. (2003). Converging evidence that stereotype threat reduces working memory capacity. *Journal of Personality and Social Psychology, 85,* 440-452.
10. von Hippel, C., Wiryakusuma, C., Bowden, J., & Schocet, M. (2011). Stereotype threat and female communication styles. *Personality and Social Psychology Bulletin, 37*(10), 1312-1324.
11. Holleran, S., Whitehead, J., Schmader, T., & Mehl, M. (2011). Talking shop and shooting the breeze: Predicting women's job disengagement from workplace conversations. *Social Psychological and Personality Science, 2,* 65-71.
12. Hall, W., Schmader, T., & Croft, E. (2013). Engineering equality: How negative interactions undermine the health and well-being of male and female engineers. In Paper presented at Society for Personality and Social Psychology Annual Meeting, New Orleans, LA, USA. (p. 149, B93).
13. Bell, A. E., Spencer, S. J., Iserman, E., & Logel, C. R. (2003). Stereotype threat and women's performance in engineering. *Journal of Engineering Education, 92*(4), 307-312.
14. Johns, M., Schmader, T., & Martens, A. (2005). Knowing is half the battle: Teaching stereotype threat as a means of improving women's math performance. *Psychological Science,16,* 175-179.
15. Aronson, J., & Williams, J. (2004). Stereotype threat: Forewarned is forearmed. Unpublished manuscript, New York University, New York.
16. Schmader, T., Johns, M., & Forbes, C. (2008). An integrated process model of stereotype threat effects on performance. *Psychological Review, 115*(2), 336-356.
17. Johns, M.J., Inzlicht, M., & Schmader, T. (2008). Stereotype threat and executive resource depletion: Examining the influence of emotion regulation. *Journal of Experimental Psychology: General, 137,* 691-705.
18. Nguyen, H.-H. D., & Ryan, A. M. (2008). Does stereotype threat affect test performance of minorities and women? A meta-analysis of experimental evidence. *Journal of Applied Psychology, 93,* 1314-1334.
19. Schmader, T. (2010). Stereotype threat deconstructed. *Current Directions in Psychological Science, 19,* 14-18.
20. Dasgupta, N., & Asgari, S. (2004). Seeing is believing: Exposure to counterstereotypic women leaders and its effect on automatic gender stereotyping. *Journal of Experimental Social Psychology, 40,* 642-658
21. Cohen, G. L., Garcia, J., Apfel, N., & Master, A. (2006). Reducing the racial achievement gap: A social-psychological intervention. *Science, 313,* 1307-1310.

Recommended Readings

1. http://www.reducingstereotypethreat.org/
2. Dr. Toni Schmader's website: http://schmader.psych.ubc.ca/research.html

Perspective References

1. Inzlicht, M., & Schmader, T. (2012). Stereotype threat: Theory, process, and application. New York, NY, US: Oxford University Press.
2. Murphy, M. C., Steele, C. M., & Gross, J. J. (2007). Signaling threat: How situational cues affect women in math, science, and engineering settings. Psychological Science, 18(10), 879-885. doi:10.1111/j.1467-9280.2007.01995.
3. Walton, G. M., & Spencer, S. J. (2009). Latent ability: Grades and test scores systematically underestimate the intellectual ability of negatively stereotyped students. Psychological Science, 20(9), 1132-1139. doi:10.1111/j.1467-9280.2009.02417.
4. Leslie, S. J., Cimpian, A., Meyer, M., & Freeland, E. (2015). Expectations of brilliance underlie gender distributions across academic disciplines. Science, 347(6219), 262–265.
5. Good, C., Aronson, J., & Inzlicht, M. (2003). Improving adolescents' standardized test performance: An intervention to reduce the effects of stereotype threat. Journal Of Applied Developmental Psychology, 24(6), 645-662. doi:10.1016/j.appdev.2003.09.002
6. Diekman, A. B., Clark, E. K., Johnston, A. M., Brown, E. R., & Steinberg, M. (2011). Malleability in communal goals and beliefs influences attraction to STEM careers: Evidence for a goal congruity perspective. Journal Of Personality And Social Psychology, 101(5), 902-918. doi:10.1037/a0025199
7. Stout, J. G., Dasgupta, N., Hunsinger, M., & McManus, M. A. (2011). STEMing the tide: Using ingroup experts to inoculate women's self-concept in science, technology, engineering, and mathematics (STEM). Journal Of Personality And Social Psychology, 100(2), 255-270. doi:10.1037/a0021385
8. Dasgupta, N., Scircle, M. M., & Hunsinger, M. (2015). Female peers in small work groups enhance women's motivation, verbal participation, and career aspirations in engineering. PNAS Proceedings Of The National Academy Of Sciences Of The United States Of America, 112(16), 4988-4993. doi:10.1073/pnas.1422822112
9. Johns, M., Schmader, T., & Martens, A. (2005). Knowing Is Half the Battle: Teaching Stereotype Threat as a Means of Improving Women's Math Performance. Psychological Science, 16(3), 175-179. doi:10.1111/j.0956-7976.2005.00799.x

Reducing Stereotype Threat

Dr. Toni Schmader
Professor, UBC Department of Psychology
Canada Research Chair in Social Psychology

Anyone can experience the discomfort of feeling that anything they say or do will be judged in terms of negative stereotypes about their group. This experience, known as stereotype threat, can be cued by seemingly innocuous features of the environment that merely bring presumptions of inability to mind.[1] For women trying to excel in science and engineering, the mere absence of other women in the workplace or the classroom has the potential to subtly suggest that women are not expected to excel.[2] In one recent meta-analysis, this experience of stereotype threat explains some of the gender gap that is often found in standardized mathematical testing as these tests are often underestimates of women's true ability.[3] Here are a few suggestions for how educators and managers can use the knowledge of this phenomena to combat its effects by creating "identity safe" environments.

Framing the game as one of skill not talent

In your field, do you think that success requires natural ability or is learned through effort? Recent research reveals that women are more underrepresented in disciplines where success is believed to be linked to genius.[4] Emphasizing that expertise is learned through mastery has been shown to improve performance for women and minorities.[5] When some groups are stereotyped to have less ability, an emphasis on uncovering natural abilities can easily feel exclusive to women and minorities.

Framing the value of the career to others

When asked why they became interested in engineering, many engineers cite their interest in solving problems and design. In practice, these skills are often carried out collaboratively to serve a broader goal that will benefit others. Because women (but also many men) tend to place higher value on helping others and not only themselves, women are more attracted to careers in science and technology when the prosocial aspects of the career are clear, and when competition amongst peers takes a backseat to collaboration as the path to excellence.[6]

Creating identity safety

In the classroom, the office, and in the field, simple things like the pronouns used, the images on websites, and the availability of smaller-sized safety equipment can signal to women that they belong.[2] To create identity safety, instructors and managers can be proactive in including positive examples of successful women in their field and establishing mentoring relationships with these women.[7] New research suggests that putting women together in groups (rather than making each a token) allows those women to find their voice, share their opinions more readily, and excel.[8]

Knowledge is power

We are all exposed to ways in which engineering gets linked more to men than to women. Just as everyone has a shared responsibility to create a work environment that is physically safe, both men and women can have a shared responsibility to recognize places where these implicit biases can creep in and call it out in themselves and others when they see it. Learning about these biases can be a powerful weapon and can inoculate women against stereotype threat.[9]

On Social Identity Threat

When our industrial advisory asked for concrete information on BC and Canadian workplaces, Dr. Croft and WWEST formed a research collaboration with Dr. Toni Schmader, Professor and Canada Research Chair in Social Psychology at the University of British Columbia, and doctoral student William Hall. They studied male and female engineers, focusing on their daily conversations. They found that daily social identity threat predicted mental exhaustion and psychological burnout. A potential solution? All employees feel more accepted and competent in workplaces with gender-inclusive policies.

"Social Identity Threat and The Workplace" is derived from this research.

Social Identity Threat & The Workplace

Social identity threat

is an anxiety or concern people experience in situations where their social group is underrepresented, devalued, or stereotyped to be inferior.[1,2]

This can be subtly triggered through conversations, or other interactions with peers and colleagues.

Social identity threat can be experienced when taking a challenging academic test, and results in poor performance on the test (known as stereotype threat[3,4]).

Why Does This Matter for STEM Professions?

STEM fields have low representation, and a high attrition rate of women.[6] For example, 11.7% of licensed engineers in Canada are women,[7] and women are leaving the profession at a higher rate than men.[8]

STEM fields, particularly engineering, often involve a lot of collaboration between coworkers. Research has shown that for female engineers, work conversations with male colleagues can be a source of social identity threat and can lead to psychological burnout.[1]

Actively addressing subtle behaviours that trigger social identity threat are critical steps in creating inclusive and safe workplaces, and retaining more women in STEM fields. This can be done through raising awareness about social identity threat, and creating spaces that welcome all identities.

Gender inclusive policies can result in all employees feeling more accepted and competent in daily conversations, and more engaged in their work.

Can Conversations Cue Social Identity Threat?

When we share ideas with others, we are **vulnerable** to a variety of responses.

Negative responses (critiques, dismissals) can trigger feelings of **incompetence** and **lack of belonging**.

When you belong to an unrepresented group, either of these feelings can cause social identity threat.

Psychological Burnout

affects individuals & organizations.

Often involves personal:[5]
- **Exhaustion**
- **Disengagement**
- **Inefficacy**

Negatively impacts **mental health**[5]

Reduces **organizational productivity**[5]

Predicts **employee turnover**[5]

The Workplace Study[1]

Pairs of engineers who work together documented **daily conversations** at work.

Findings

Anxiety
"I don't belong here"
Incompetence

On days when a conversation with a male colleague cued feelings of incompetence and a lack of acceptance...

For men: no change in social identity threat levels

For women: higher levels of social identity threat

Women reported experiencing **more daily social identity threat** than their male colleagues, predicting:

mental exhaustion & **psychological burnout.**

All employees feel more accepted and competent in daily conversations in workplaces with **gender inclusive policies.**

References

1. Hall, W., Schmader, T., & Croft, E. (2015). Engineering exchanges: Daily social identity threat predicts burnout among female engineers. *Social Psychology and Personality Science, 6*(5), 528-534.

2. Steele, C., Spencer, S., & Aronson, J. (2002). Contending with group image: The psychology of stereotype and social identity threat. *Advances in Experimental Social Psychology, 34*, 379–440.

3. Schmader, T., Johns, M., & Forbes, C. (2008). An integrated process model of stereotype threat effects on performance. *Psychological Review, 115*, 336–356.

4. Steele, C. M. (1999, August). Thin ice: Stereotype threat and black college students. *The Atlantic Monthly*, 28, 44–47, 50–54.

5. Maslach, C., Schaufeli, W. B., & Leiter, M. P. (2001). Job burnout. *Annual Review of Psychology, 52*, 397–422.

6. Hill, C., Corbett, C., & St. Rose, A. (2013). *Why so few?: Women in science, technology, engineering and mathematics.* Washington, DC: AAUW.

7. Engineers Canada. (2014). *2013 Membership survey*. Retrieved from http://www.engineerscanada.ca/national-membership-report/

8. Hunt, J. (2010). Why do women leave science and engineering? (NBER Working paper 15853). Cambridge, MA: National Bureau of Economic Research.

Recommended Readings

1. http://www.reducingstereotypethreat.org/

Shared Experience

Ms. Catherine Roome, P.Eng.
President & CEO, BC Safety Authority

What worked in my case – to both attract me to a career in STEM and keep me there – was having a group of people around me who were in a similar place in their lives. A person once said to me "we all have to go through the same steps in life… everyone of us. It's the winners though, who simply get through the bad experiences faster". So every time something was a bump in my road, having the ability to talk about how to handle it or reflecting after the fact with my community of peers with shared experience, was incredibly powerful. And it is this group of women who have been through it with me, who are now also continuing to provide the same support for the generation after us who are looking for careers in STEM.

I will continue to advocate that women in STEM need networks of support. We need to work at keeping those connections alive, and we need that lifeline of shared experience so that we are not only resilient, but that we use the support and optimism of others to help us thrive!

The other day I shared this experience with my daughter:

Over 15 years ago I was starting a new role – moving from the technical campus of a very large energy company to their corporate office – and I knew at that precise moment that this was the beginning of my leadership career as an engineer. I had set up a new child care arrangement for my two pre-school age children, worked out the commute, prepared my daily schedule to manage the change and was wearing a smart new outfit for my first day. I arrived 25 minutes early and found my desk. As I settled myself in and felt my adrenaline taper off, I started to notice more around me. I noticed my new dress. And I noticed that I had forgotten to put on a bra. Seriously. I can laugh about it now.

I shared this experience with my nineteen year old daughter because she has just started electrical biomedical studies in engineering. She has just moved into a new apartment, organized, furnished and decorated it, and she has had her timetable planned to the minute. Last week she arrived for the first day of classes for her second year term and realized within 5 minutes she hadn't brought a single thing to write with. Not a pen, a pencil, her laptop – nothing. Seriously. She was laughing about it.

We go like crazy and we prepare. And inevitably something falls through the cracks. Resilience allows us to shake things off and keep going. Shared experiences ingrain that message of strength and allow us to thrive.

And being able to laugh about it helps.

On Diversity for Managers

Diversity breeds innovation. Attracting and retaining a diverse talent pool is a competitive advantage, as a diverse team brings more ideas and perspectives to the table. As a manager, you can make a difference by demonstrating that you value your employees and you value their diversity. Create people-friendly policies and encourage all members of your team to develop and expand their skills. Encourage team members to step to leadership positions and take on new challenges. A good first step? Review the people-friendly policies your company offers and ensure that they are truly available – a policy an employee feels they cannot use is worse than no policy at all.

Understanding Workplace Diversity
For Managers

In a blind resume study, male candidates were offered higher salaries, more mentorship, and were rated as more "**competent**" and "**hireable**," than women, despite the candidates' resumes being identical.[17]

Several issues need to be addressed to **retain a diverse workforce**. The "old white boys' club"[3] that excludes others from informal networking, a lack of managerial awareness about diversity issues, poor work-life balance, and discriminatory behaviours against minority employees can dissuade all workers from being loyal to an employer in the long term.[3,19]

Promoting diversity is not limited to gender; workplaces should be inclusive and welcoming to all.

The benefits of creating an inclusive workplace include low turnover, higher employee engagement, improved client relationships and satisfaction, stronger fiscal performance, and improved governance.[4,5,6]

This paper highlights eight ways to recruit, support and retain a diverse workforce in organizations.

See work-life balance as an **investment** in your employees[4]

Offer **family-friendly** policies[10]

What policies does your organization have?

Create and maintain clear policies on

promotions, retention, and work/life balance,
and **communicate** them to all employees

 Flexible scheduling is vital for retaining **mid-career women**[1] and valuable to **all** employees[15]

Clear, **well-documented**, and **equitable** promotion and retention policies reduce **significant gender gaps**[8]

? ?   Promoted

Which ones are priorities for your organization?

Better management performance[22,23]

Share priorities with staff, stakeholders & investors

Priorities

Understand and communicate the business case for diversity
in your organization

Access to a **broader talent base**[26]

Increased **innovation** capacity[24,25]

Stronger **financial** performance[20,21,22]

16% higher Return on Sales[20]

Fortune 500 companies with more women on average perform better[20]

26% higher Return on Invested Capital[20]

Negative interpersonal experiences at work predicted **lower organizational commitment** and **life satisfaction** for women[9]

Anxiety Isolation
Poor self-efficacy Stress
Self-conscious

Men in exclusive and stressful workplaces, report having poor physical health, including heart conditions[9]

Monitor the working climate and **foster a positive, inclusive work culture**

Have a **zero tolerance** policy for derogatory comments or actions[3]

Safe Space

Provide **professional development opportunities** for **all employees, on company time**

LGBT employees are happier at organizations with **leadership programs**[3]

Employees' workplace satisfaction

13 - 24%

With leadership development programs

Without leadership development programs

These programs also have positive effects for all employees, including more ownership, engagement, and co-operation[2]

Organizations tend to be self-replicating when hiring

Try the Implicit Bias test:
https://implicit.harvard.edu/

Identify and invite or sponsor women for **leadership positions**[6,16]

Leader Leader

20%

14%

♂ ♀

Male mid-level employees are more likely than women peers to apply for a managerial role despite **only partially** meeting the job description[13]

Become aware of your **organization's hiring tendencies** and your **subconscious biases**

Subconscious biases[†] affect **everyday decision-making processes** (hiring processes, assumptions made about others)

Set an example for embracing inclusivity in the workplace[3]

Non-traditional mentoring includes:[11]

Speed Mentoring

Virtual Mentoring

Promote and establish **Mentoring Programs**[‡]

Provides Access to:[5, 8, 12]

Knowledge
Support

Diverse Mentors

Networking

Establish structured diversity measures[7]

- ☑ Include diversity as part of all employee's reporting;
- ☑ Track diversity (ethically);[10]
- ☑ Reflect your commitment in marketing and communications;
- ☑ Report on progress

Set targets[5]

Diversity

Do a **Diversity Audit** at your organization[10]

Ensure every employee has an opportunity for advancement[3]

Assign
accountability for diversity
and track your progress[10]

Create a **culture of diversity**[10]

Build **Diversity Culture** with diversity shares at meetings

Safety?

Safety comes from a **safety culture**;
Diversity comes from a **diversity culture**

Diversity?

Think **safe**.

Think **diverse**.

Why do women leave work?

60% of highly qualified women have **nonlinear** careers[14]

Historically, **24%** of highly qualified men also have nonlinear careers[14]

75% of the Millennial generation expect to have 2-5 employers in their life[18]

Off-Ramps and On-Ramps[14]

Career

Family demands

Educational leaves

Opportunities

Toddlers
Teenagers
Elder Care

Work-life policies tend to target young children[14]

93% want to return[14]...

...only **73%** do[14]

Avg. time off work: **2.2** years[14]

Flexible hours

Part-time work

Self-employment

Some never return

Challenges:
- Salary gaps
- Negotiating a schedule

The Benefits of Change

Employees are more satisfied and committed when they have **positive work relationships** with managers and colleagues.[3] By supporting diversity, managers and organizations can foster positive work cultures for all.

Committing to change can make a difference; UBC's Faculty of Science went from having **no women** in senior leadership positions from 2003-2007 to having **5/13** senior faculty positions held by women from 2007-2010.[12]

Managers should **celebrate their successes** and be open to a wide range of communication styles.[1] While the inequality gap tends to increase over time,[8] taking direct action such as assigning accountability for diversity can lead to short and long term changes.

Training and **feedback** can be an effective method for eliminating managerial bias and inequality.[7] Opportunities for technical and leadership development need to be available to **employees of all ranks**.[1]

Allowing workers to off-ramp partially or completely and welcoming them back later **without penalty**, combating stigma and stereotypes by training staff to be self-reflective and deconstruct their own processes, and making organizational decision-making as transparent as possible helps build a **culture of diversity** within organizations.[10,14] WWEST is currently researching which specific policies best support gender diversity in the workplace.[Δ]

References

1. Simard, C., Henderson, A., Gilmartin, S., Shiebinger, L. & Whitney, T. (2008). *Climbing the technical ladder: Obstacles and solutions for mid-level women in technology.* Anita Borg Institute and Clayman Institute for Gender Research. Retrieved from http://anitaborg.org/files/Climbing_the_Technical_Ladder.pdf

2. Politt, D. (2012). Leadership programme brings big benefits for Raytheon. *Training & Management Development Methods, 26*(5), 5109-5114.

3. Silva, C. & Warren, A. (2009). *Building LGBT-inclusive workplaces: Engaging organizations and individuals in change.* Retrieved from http://www.catalyst.org/knowledge/building-lgbt-inclusive-workplaces-engaging-organizations-and-individuals-change

4. Emerson, C., Williams, F., & Sherk. S. (2000). *Best practices for the retention of women engineers and scientists in the oil and gas sector.* New Frontiers, New Traditions National Conference for the Advancement of Women in Engineering, Science & Technology. Retrieved from http://www.mun.ca/cwse/BestPractices.pdf

5. Society for Human Resource Management. (2009). *Global diversity and inclusion: perceptions, practices and attitudes.* Retrieved from http://www.shrm.org/

6. Mattis, M. (2001). Advancing women in business organizations: Key leadership roles and behaviors of senior leaders and middle managers. *Journal of Management Development, 20*(4), 371-388.

7. Kalev, A., Dobbin, F., & Kelly, E. (2006). Best practices or best guesses? Assessing the efficacy of corporate affirmative action and diversity policies. *American Sociological Review, 71*(4),589-617.

8. Kuske, R., Croft, E., Condon, A., Heckman, N, Hibsch-Jetter, C., Ingram, G., Maddison, W., McKenna, J., & van de Panne, Michiel. (2007). *An assessment of the working climate for science faculty at UBC.* Retrieved from http://science.ubc.ca/faculty/diversity

9. Hall, W., Schmader, T., & Croft, E. (2013). *Engineering equality: How negative interactions undermine the health and well-being of male and female engineers.* Paper presented at Society for Personality and Social Psychology Annual Meeting, New Orleans, LA, USA.

10. Cukier, W., Smarz, S. & Yap, M. (2012). Using the diversity audit tool to assess the status of women in the Canadian financial services sector. *The International Journal of Diversity in Organizations, Communities and Nations, 11*(3), 15-36.

11. APEGBC Women in Engineering and Geoscience Task Force. (2013). *Women in engineering and geoscience task force report.* Retrieved from http://www.apeg.bc.ca/about/wiegtf.html

12. Condon, A., Hibsch-Jetter, C., Parrish, K. & Peacock, S. (2011). *Equity and working climate initiative and outcomes pertaining to tenure-track at science: 2007-2010.* Retrieved from http://science.ubc.ca/faculty/diversity

13. Institute of Leadership & Management. (2011). *Ambition and gender at work.* Retrieved from http://www.i-l-m.com/Why-ILM/Research-reports/Ambition-and-gender

14. Hewlett, S.A. (2007). *Off-ramps and on-ramps.* Boston, MA: Harvard Business School Press.

15. Servon, L.J., & Visser, M.A. (2011). Progress hindered: the retention and advancement of women in science, engineering and technology careers. *Human Resource Management Journal, 21*(3), 272-284.

16. Davey, K. M. (2008). Women's accounts of organizational politics as a gendering process. *Gender, Work & Organization, 15,* 650–671.

17. Moss-Racusin, C. et al. (2012). Science faculty's subtle gender biases favor male students. *Proceedings of the National Academy of Sciences of the United States of America, 109*(41), 16474-16479.

18. PriceWaterhouseCoopers. (2008). *Millennial at work: Perspectives from a new generation.* Retrieved from http://www.pointconsultinggroup.com/?portfolio=managing-tomorrow%E2%80%99-people

19. Ghosh, P., Satyawadi, R., Joshi, J.P., & Shadman, M. (2013) Who stays with you? Factors predicting employees' intention to stay. *International Journal of Organizational Analysis, 21*(3), 288-312.

20. Catalyst. (2011). *The bottom line: Corporate performance and women's representation on boards (2004-2008).* Retrieved from http://www.catalyst.org/knowledge/bottom-line-corporate-performance-and-womens-representation-boards-20042008

21. Adler, R. D. (1999). *Women in the executive suite correlate to high profits.* For European Project on Equal Pay. Retrieved from http://www.w2t.se/se/filer/adler_web.pdf

22. Brown, D. A. A., Brown, D.L. & Anastasopoulos, V. (2002). *Women on boards: Not just the right thing... But the "bright" thing.* The Conference Board of Canada. Retrieved from http://www.conferenceboard.ca/

23. Orser, B. (2000). *Creating high-performance organizations: Leveraging women's leadership.* The Conference Board of Canada. Retrieved from http://www.conferenceboard.ca/

24. Torchia, M., Calabrò, A., & Huse, M. (2011). Women directors on corporate boards: From tokenism to critical mass. *Journal of Business Ethics, 102*(2), 299-317.

25. Woolley, A., Malone, T. & Berinato, (2011). What makes a team smarter? More women. *Harvard Business Review*, 89(6), 32-33. Retrieved from http://hbr.org/2011/06/defend-your-research-what-makes-a-team-smarter-more-women/ar/1

26. Mannix, E., & Neale. M.A. (2005). What differences make a difference? The promise and reality of diverse teams in organizations. *Psychological Science in the Public Interest. 6*(2), 31-55.

Recommended Readings

1. Babcock, L. & Laschever, S. (2003). *Women don't ask: Negotiation and the gender divide.* Princeton, NJ: Princeton University Press.

2. Hewlett, S. A. (2010, June). *Off-ramps and on-ramps revisited.* Harvard Business Review. Retrieved from http://hbr.org/2010/06/off-ramps-and-on-ramps-revisited/ar/1

† WWEST. (2013). *Unconscious Bias.* Retrieved from http://wwest.mech.ubc.ca/diversity/

‡ WWEST. (2013). *Mentoring Works.* Retrieved from http://wwest.mech.ubc.ca/diversity/

Δ For more information, please see Engendering Engineering Success: http://wwest.mech.ubc.ca/ees/

Workplace Diversity for Managers

Ms. Courtnay Hughes, M.ASc.
Manager, HR Research, Mining Industry Human Resources Council

The business case for creating a more diverse and inclusive workforce is compelling, proven by extensive and vigorous research, and enacted in numerous successful organizations. Despite this, managers find it difficult to carve out time to engage in diversity and inclusion. To change this narrative, diversity and inclusion must progress from a specific initiative or program into something that permeates all aspects of business. This involves using a critical eye to assess bias (ours and others'), then making changes to remove barriers to inclusion. In the same way we embody safety culture into STEM organizations, we need to integrate diversity and inclusion into the value systems and cultures of our organizations.

Managers in STEM fields have a unique responsibility to both their team and to senior leaders. They provide the organizational pulse to senior leaders, and can make tactical change that ensures inclusion is personified within organizations.

Recruitment is a good starting place to understand and assess your organization's diversity. Identifying biases within hiring frameworks can be as simple as asking a few key questions:

- Are we engaging with organizations or associations that support diversity groups?
- Is there any language or imagery in our advertisements that is not inclusive?
- When hiring internally are we encouraging women to apply for leadership roles/stretch assignments etc.?
- Are there areas in our organization (location, specific teams, senior leadership) where there is a blaring gender gap?

Answering these questions can highlight barriers that exist and lead to mitigations such as: using inclusive imagery on company advertisements; ensuring hiring panels are diverse; removing names on applications to prevent bias; and having greater awareness of organizational gender gaps and diverse high potential employees.

Diversifying a workforce doesn't stop with hiring, from a manager's perspective developing and retaining high performing employees is equally important. Scanning your organizations' employment policies and assessing their depth and application can uncover inclusion barriers that may be leading to turnover, or retention challenges.

To assess organizational employment policies, ask:
- Are there policy and procedures in place to address harassment, bullying and violence in the workplace?
- Does our organization offer flexible work arrangements or telecommuting options?
- When working in remote locations or the field, have we addressed personal safety issues that are gender specific?
- Are there appropriate sizes of Personal Protective Equipment (PPE) for all employees' at all operational sites?

Identifying the intention and assessing the application of policies within your team and broader organization is the next step to ensuring that a policy isn't conflicting with a workplace culture or value system. For an organization to exemplify inclusion it is critical that all policies apply to all employees, at all levels, and in all work settings within the organization.

Managers play an important role in building a diversity culture within organizations. They can support greater inclusion by evaluating the application of employment policies and programs within their teams and raise awareness of inconsistencies uncovered to senior leaders. Managers are attuned to both the tactical and strategic aspects of workplaces and are well positioned to drive real change in organizations.

On Gendered Language and Hiring

Hiring can be arduous. Finding a person with the right skills and experience that shares your company's values is a challenge, but it is also an opportunity to bring new skills and perspectives to your team. To maximize this opportunity, it is essential to attract a broad talent pool and find objective ways to select – and then secure – the best candidate. We know from the business case that innovation is maximized when you have a diverse team, but organizations tend to be self-replicating unless you make a conscious effort to be inclusive in recruitment and selection. Where to start? The next time you hire, consider blinding the applications. Before distributing resumes for review replace names with ID numbers and black out any pronouns.

Gendered Language & Stereotype Awareness
for Hiring Committees

In a hiring process, stereotypes, unconscious bias and communication styles can **unknowingly influence** impressions of candidates and jobs.

Women's behaviour tends to be stereotyped as **communal** (kind, thoughtful, sensitive to others' feelings, deferent), whereas men are stereotyped as **agentic** (competitive, decisive, aggressive, socially dominant).[1] Women also are encouraged to be more self-assertive, but discouraged from advancing their interests at the cost of others.[1]

Language can also be characterized as **feminine** or **masculine**; being more indirect, elaborate and emotional for the former, or more succinct, direct and instrumental for the latter.[2]

These stereotypes and assumptions can impact a hiring committee's assessment of a **candidate's abilities**, as well as the candidate's assessment of a job description and **their "fit"** within an organization.

Job ads with masculine language are **less appealing** to women, regardless of job type, and decreased their **anticipated belonging** to the organization.[3] Conversely, gendered language had **no impact** on men's anticipated belonging.[3]

Gender Discrimination Exists

Gender segregation is the tendency for women to work in **systematically different occupations** and industries than men.[4] This often occurs at **critical career points**, which can dissuade women from continuing in male-dominated industries.[3]

Women grow more aware of the "**glass ceiling**" as they advance in their careers:

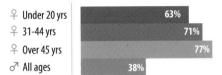

♀ Under 20 yrs — 63%
♀ 31-44 yrs — 71%
♀ Over 45 yrs — 77%
♂ All ages — 38%

Percentage of workers who believe barriers that prevent women from reaching management level exist[6]

Women with children experienced **declines in earnings** and **hours worked**; men with children correlated with **increased earnings** and **virtually unchanged hours**.[5]

Stereotypes & Their Effects

Stereotype: Men

Agentic:
competitive
decisive
aggressive
socially dominant

Stereotype: Women

Communal:
kind
thoughtful
sensitive to others
deferent

Traditionally, companies have valued agentic behaviour over communal behaviour

Agentic women are stereotyped as **competent**, but **interpersonally insensitive**.[7]

This is used to **justify** keeping them out of **male-dominated** management positions.[1,3]

Some women counteract negative stereotypes by adopting a more masculine communication style.[2] This can be effective for some women, but not all. Agentic behaviours have social costs.[2]

Word Choice Matters

Gendered wording **subtly** signals who **belongs** and **who doesn't**. Below are examples of language in job advertisements and qualities of candidates.

Feminine

- a company's "**excellence**" in the market[3]
- "**understand** markets to **establish** appropriate selling prices"[3]
- "We are **committed** to providing top quality health care that is **sympathetic** to the needs or our patients"[3]

MASCULINE

- a company's "**dominance**" in the market[3]
- "**analyze** markets to **determine** appropriate selling prices"[3]
- "We are **determined** to deliver **superior** medical treatment tailored to each individual patient"[3]

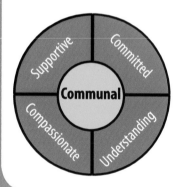

Women in Leadership Positions

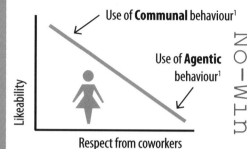

No-Win

Both actions carry a risk of being disqualified from a job application.[1]

Observed Effects of Women Using Forced Agentic Behaviour

⬆ Increase ♀'s **competence scores** to equally agentic men[1]

⬇ Seem more **threatening;** less **persuasive** & less **influential**[2]

⬇ Decrease **compliance** of workers for ♀ managers[2]

If women need to manage the impressions they give off, it can lead to **stress, anxiety and reduced task performance.**[2,3]

Gendered language has **no impact** on men's decision to apply, but may dissuade women.[3]

It also goes **unnoticed** in job advertisements; even when explicitly pointed out.[3]

Gendered Job Descriptions[3]
For an Engineer

Feminine	MASCULINE
"**Proficient** oral and written communication skills"[3]	"**Strong** communication and influencing skills"[3]
"Collaborates well, in a **team** environment"[3]	"Ability to **perform individually** in a **competitive** environment"[3]
"**Sensitive** to the clients' needs, can **develop warm** client relationships"[3]	"**Superior** ability to **satisfy** customers and **manage** company's association with them"[3]
"Provide general **support** to project teams in a manner complimentary to the company"[3]	"**Direct** project groups to **manage** project **progress** and **ensure** accurate task **control**"[3]

"Qualified"

Only partially meet the advertised job requirements?

Men are more likely to apply, regardless.[6]

85% of women would only apply to a job if they met the job description **"fully"** or **"pretty well."**[6]

Women are also less likely to apply for masculine-stereotyped jobs.[4]

Deciding to Apply

Identification with the Job

(is it consistent with the individual's identity?)

Reward Preference

Expectation of Application Success

(financial, intellectual, schedule flexibility, etc)

Men and women evaluate job decision factors differently because of **gender role socialization.**[4]

What Can We Do?

Gendered language is not a deliberate process - most job ads only contain 1% gendered language[3] – but impact women's application decisions. Increasing **feminine language** in job descriptions can **increase women's interest** in the job.[7]

Organizations need to rethink their hiring process, and should ensure career advancement **reflects skills and capabilities** instead of emphasizing time served.[6] When attracting women to a job, **flexible working hours** and **work-life balance** are important,[4] as well as ensuring they have a **sense of anticipated belonging** in the organization.[3] In the study of MBA graduates, women were no less likely to receive offers in masculine jobs; the segregation occurred in the application process where **women self-selected the jobs** they believed they fit.[4]

Women's leadership potential should be maximized through **professional development**, **mentoring**, and **proactively identifying** talented individuals and encouraging them to apply for upper level jobs.[6] The negative effects of communal communication stereotypes can also be eliminated through **self-affirmation exercises.**[2]

Interview Best Practices[4]

Is this what I want to do?

Job technical and skill requirements

What benefits do you offer? Vacation, childcare, flextime, insurance, professional development, mentoring?

Compensation, including work-life balance provisions

Go beyond the technical details and salary discussions

Working relationships and workplace climate

Will there be people like me?

Expectations for availability and travel

How do current employees handle family demands?

Interview best practices help you find the best employee, and are **universally helpful, regardless of gender**.[10,12] Lifestyle and workplace climate discussions are particularly important to women[9] and young workers[8, 11] (Millennials / Gen Y).

References

1. Rudman, L. & Glick, P. (2001). Prescriptive gender stereotypes and backlash toward agentic women. *Journal of Social Issues, 57*(4), 743-762.

2. von Hippel, C. Wiryakusuma, C., Bowden, J. & Shochet, M. (2011). Stereotype threat and female communication styles. *Personality and Social Psychology Bulletin, 37*(10), 1312-1324.

3. Gaucher, D., Friesen, J. & Kay, A. (2011). Evidence that gendered wording in job advertisements exists and sustains gender inequality. *Journal of Personality and Social Psychology, 101*(1), 109-128.

4. Barbulescu, R. & Bidwell, M. (2013). Do women choose different jobs from men? *Organization Science, 24*(3), 737-756.

5. Bertrand, M., Goldin, C., Katz, L. F. (2009). Dynamics of the gender gap for young professionals in the corporate and financial sectors. *NBER Working Paper, 14681*. Retrieved from http://www.nber.org/papers/w14681

6. Institute of Leadership & Management. (2011). *Ambition and gender at work.* Retrieved from http://www.i-l-m.com/Why-ILM/Research-reports/Ambition-and-gender

7. Rudman, L. & Glick, P. (1999). Feminized management and backlash toward agentic women: The hidden cost to women of a kinder, gentler image of middle managers. *Journal of Personality and Social Psychology, 77*(5), 1004-1010.

8. Ng, E., Schweitzer, L., & Lyons, S. (2010). New generation, great expectations: A field study of the millennial generation. *Journal of Business and Psychology, 25*(2), 281-292.

9. Simard, C., Henderson, A., Gilmartin, S., Shiebinger, L. & Whitney, T. (2008). *Climbing the technical ladder: Obstacles and solutions for mid-level women in technology.* Anita Borg Institute and Clayman Institute for Gender Research. Retrieved from http://anitaborg.org/files/Climbing_the_Technical_Ladder.pdf

10. Robak, J.C. (2007). Employer of choice: Attracting high-performance talent. *Journal (American Water Works Association), 99*(8), 22-24, 27-28.

11. Terjesen, S., Vinnicombe, S., & Freeman, C. (2007). Attracting Generation Y graduates: Organisational attributes, likelihood to apply and sex differences. *Career Development International, 12*(6), 504-522.

12. McGinn, K.L. & Milkman, K.L. (2013). Looking up and looking out: Career mobility effects of demographic similarity among professionals. *Organization Science, 24*(4), 1041-1060.

Recommended Readings

1. Heilman, M. E. (2001). Description and prescription: How gender stereotypes prevent women's ascent up the organizational ladder. *Journal of Social Issues, 57*, 657-674.

2. Eagly, A. H., & Carli, L. L. (2003). The female leadership advantage: An evaluation of the evidence. *Leadership Quarterly, 14*, 807-834.

3. Eagly, A. H., & Karau, S.J. (2002). Role congruity theory of prejudice toward female leaders. *Psychological Review, 109*, 573-598.

4. Cejka, M. A., & Eagly, A. H. (1999). Gender-stereotypic images of occupations correspond to the sex segregation of employment. *Personality & Social Psychology Bulletin, 35*(4), 413-423.

5. http://www.reducingstereotypethreat.org/

Gendered Words in Job Advertisements

Gendered wording **subtly** signals who **belongs** and **who doesn't**. Below are examples of language in job advertisements and qualities of candidates.

Feminine

- a company's "**excellence**" in the market
- "**understand** markets to **establish** appropriate selling prices"
- "We are **committed** to providing top quality health care that is **sympathetic** to the needs or our patients"

MASCULINE

- a company's "**dominance**" in the market
- "**analyze** markets to **determine** appropriate selling prices"
- "We are **determined** to deliver **superior** medical treatment tailored to each individual patient"

Source:
Gaucher, D., Friesen, J. & Kay, A. (2011). Evidence that gendered wording in job advertisements exists and sustains gender inequality. *Journal of Personality and Social Psychology, 101*(1), 109-128.

Sample Gendered Words

Feminine	MASCULINE
Affectionate	Active
Cheer*	Adventurous
Commit*	Aggress*
Communal	Ambitio*
Compassion*	Analy*
Connect*	Assert*
Considerate	Athlet*
Cooperat*	Autonom*
Depend*	Challeng*
Emotiona*	Compet*
Empath*	Confident
Flatterable	Courag*
Gentle	Decide
Honest	Decisive
Interdependen*	Decision*
Interpersona*	Determin*
Kind	Domina*
Kinship	Force*
Loyal*	Hierarch*
Nurtur*	Hostil*
Pleasant*	Independen*
Polite	Individual*
Quiet*	Intellect*
Respon*	Lead*
Sensitiv*	Logic
Submissive	Objective
Support*	Opinion
Sympath*	Outspoken
Tender*	Persist
Together*	Principle*
Trust*	Stubborn
Understand*	Superior
Warm*	Self-confiden*
Yield*	Self-sufficien*
	Self-relian*

* indicates a wildcard where the program used in the research captured a variety of word endings

Perspective References

1. Engineers Canada. (2014). *Canadian Engineers for Tomorrow: Trends in Engineering Enrolment and Degrees Awarded 2009-2013*. Retrieved from http://www.engineerscanada.ca/enrolment-and-degrees-awarded-report

2. Gaucher, D., Friesen, J. & Kay, A. (2011). Evidence that gendered wording in job advertisements exists and sustains gender inequality. *Journal of Personality and Social Psychology, 101*(1), 109-128.

3. d'Entremont, A.G., Greer, K., & Lyon, K.A. (2015). Gendered Words in Canadian Engineering Recruitment Documents. In N. Saleh (Ed.), *2015 Proceedings of the Canadian Engineering Education Association (CEEA) Conference: 2015 McMaster University* (pp. 1-7). Kingston: Queen's University Press.

Creating an (Un)inviting Environment Through Texts & Images: Representations of Gender in Engineering Recruitment Materials

Dr. Kerry Greer
Instructor, UBC
Department of Sociology

Dr. Agnes d'Entremont
Instructor, UBC Department
of Mechanical Engineering

Ms. Katherine Lyon, M.A.
Ph.D. Candidate, UBC
Department of Sociology

Ms. Dianna Demmers
B.A.Sc. Candidate, UBC
Department of Civil Engineering

Women students experience an overwhelmingly male class environment in Engineering departments when they arrive on campus, but even before they begin university, women encounter masculine-dominated language in the way universities in Canada talk about engineering in their recruitment materials. Our research looks to see if this is counter-balanced by emphasizing women's presence in recruitment photos. Preliminary findings suggest that women are often overrepresented in recruitment material images, suggesting that universities are aware of their need to highlight the presence of women in order to recruit more women students into engineering.

With the proportion of tenure track women faculty in engineering ranging from a low of zero percent to a high of 25 percent (among the 18 Canadian engineering programs in our study), and the proportion of undergraduate women students ranging from a low of 5 percent to a high of 29 percent,[1] women students are a minority. Even before they apply for engineering programs, however, women students are confronted by an onslaught of language describing these programs using words that research shows are perceived to be associated with masculinity and men's spaces.[2] Less than one-third of the total words that are "gendered" are female-associated.[3] These numbers become even more unbalanced when we look at specific disciplines within Engineering. While some disciplines achieve parity between language perceived to be masculine and feminine (such as in Material Engineering), Engineering Physics uses no feminine-associated words.

While the texts women read describing the programs they aspire to join tend to be masculine-associated, in the accompanying photographs women are disproportionately present in our research sample. On average 18 percent of students in engineering are women, however program materials featured images of women 30 percent of the time on recruitment websites. Comparing gender representation in images across disciplines we found that some programs feature images of women at a rate similar to the number of women in these specific disciplines (Biosystems, Chemical, Mechanical), but overall the trend is to include a disproportionate number of women in recruitment website photos. For instance, Engineering Physics, which has 14 percent women student enrollees, featured women in images half the time.

What are the consequences of over-representing women, beyond highlighting their presence to encourage more women to join them? Spotlight bias is a term adopted from social psychology that refers to the feeling that too many people pay attention to us when we stand out in some way. In the case of gender recruitment into university, we theorize that placing too much emphasis on women's visibility in departments, especially when it is not reflective of the number of women actually enrolled, creates a context in which women feel singled out. We wonder if this might make women students feel they represent a group who "do not belong" in engineering.

On Mentoring

When you walk through the forest, every path has forks and branches, side trails, and places to simply sit and enjoy the surroundings. Career paths are much the same. And if you examine each decision point – whether you turn or go straight, take a moment or keep going – you may realize that you never make those decisions in a vacuum. In addition to your travelling companions, there might be other people on the path, maps, or a glimpse of a beautiful vista. In your career, these guides are often people around you – your mentors. Mentors can be formal or informal; you might meet them once or you might become long-term friends. Some mentors might be like the others on the path, people you pass or walk with for a short time, exchanging information. Some might be like the map, people who has travelled the path you want to follow. Some might be like the glimpse of a vista, an inspirational person you chance to meet. Some will be your travelling companions: your peers, your coworkers, your supervisor, and your supports. These mentors have a significant impact on both the path you take and how happy you are on your journey – seek out these relationships, and care for them.

Mentoring Works

Why Mentoring?

Women who have a mentor can advance more quickly, and to higher levels, than those who are not supported.[3]

Mentoring relationships can be formal or informal, and short or long term.

Formal relationships are often arranged by an organization or workplace, have pre-articulated expectations, and often include launches, wrap-ups, and socials to normalize expectations. Formal mentorships create an environment where it is easy to get involved, but may cause concerns of time commitment and how "visible" the relationships are.

Informal mentoring is often arranged by individuals, so expectations are not always pre-determined and must be set by the mentor and mentee. They often focus on a specific need. Time commitments are more flexible, and informal mentorship is less "visible." Difficulty establishing connections can make it challenging to become involved.

Short term mentoring formats include speed mentoring, project-specific mentors, shadowing, or transition mentors.

Long term mentoring may include regular or ad-hoc meetings, peer mentors, and most mentoring programs. Online mentoring may use either format.

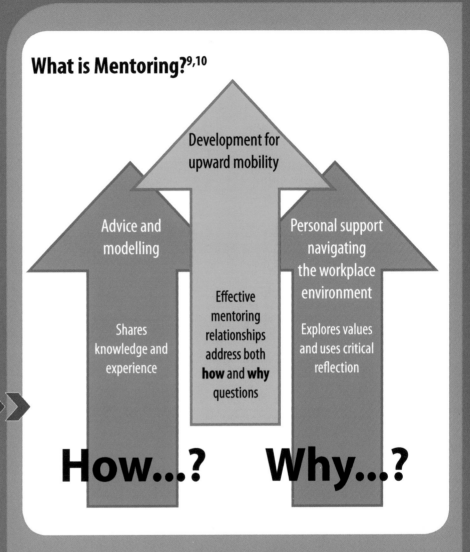

What is Mentoring?[9,10]

Development for upward mobility

Advice and modelling

Shares knowledge and experience

Effective mentoring relationships address both **how** and **why** questions

Personal support navigating the workplace environment

Explores values and uses critical reflection

How...?   Why...?

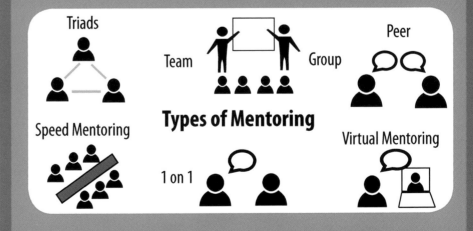

Types of Mentoring

Triads

Team

Group

Peer

Speed Mentoring

1 on 1

Virtual Mentoring

Ranked Facilitative Responses[2]

Reflecting & Understanding Feelings — Conveys you have heard and understood their emotional experience

Clarifying & Summarizing — Focuses the discussion; indicates accurate hearing & understanding

Indicates a desire to be accurate in communication

Questioning — Seeks information & furthers discussion

Reassuring & Supporting — May dismiss the person's feelings (negative)

Indicates a belief in their ability to solve the problem

Analyzing & Interpreting — Trying to explain behaviours or feelings

Responses may imply what they should think or do

Advising — What you should do or feel

Evaluating — Judges what you do or feel

In a mentoring relationship, **how you respond** affects how the other person responds. Choosing a response is context and relationship dependent.

Facilitative Conditions[1]

Friendliness	Sharing mutual interests	Genuine warmth	Genuine sense of comfort and support

Understanding	Empathy	Perceive and acknowledge their experiences

Caring	Value them as a person	Personal commitment to the process	Personally care about their well-being

Respect	Right to express their own ideas and feelings	Right to shape their own lives

Trustworthiness	Confidentiality and security in relationship	Honesty

Acceptance	Accept who they are	Respect the personal worth and dignity of a person

6 conditions must be met to create a relationship in which a person feels **comfortable to self-disclose.**[1]
In a mentorship, this relationship is **reciprocal.**

Types of Questions

Effective:
- Are person-centred
- Are **open**
- Ask "**why**" (without being intimidating)

Ineffective:
- Completely change the focus
- Are binding
- Solicit agreement
- Force choices
- Have "no good answer"
- Are yes/no

Tools for Mentoring[4,5]

Preparing for Mentoring

Decide what you want to get from this experience

Determine **what you can give** (time, knowledge) and **what you can't** (things you won't discuss)

Know your own **values**

Review the **facilitative responses**

Decide on **3 questions** you want to ask

Setting Expectations

Set & communicate **expectations** (meetings, forms of communication, etc.)

Discuss any **limitations** to the relationship, **confidentiality**, what to do if one person wants to end the relationship

Write this into a **simple agreement**

Building the Facilitative Conditions

Find **common ground** (personal, professional interests)

Leave the workplace – go for a walk, or for coffee

Use **open questions** & positive body language

Talk about why mentoring **appeals to you**, previous valuable mentoring relationships you've had, and **how they were helpful**

Tools to Explore

Choose a **specific topic** to focus on for each individual session

Have the mentee create a pie chart of what is **important** in their life, then create one of what they spend their time on – compare & discuss

Approach issues with **PEST analysis**: Political, Economic, Social, Technology

Tools to Reflect

Review **highlights** from the meeting at the end

At home, spend **15 minutes** writing about what you learned, what was helpful, what you'd like to do next time

At the end of the mentoring relationship, or yearly, reflect on **how it has contributed** to your growth and development

Mentoring at Work

Increasing workplace diversity, especially at the mid- and upper levels, can be supported through diversity mentoring programs.[8] Organizations should also consider how to promote and support a variety of forms of mentoring, and reduce barriers to employees' participation.

Often, individuals who need mentoring the most are unable to find mentors because they are afraid to ask, or are searching for the "perfect fit" mentor.[7] Informal mentoring can help resolve this. Peer mentoring is also beneficial; individuals with similar levels of experience act as both mentees and mentors to each other,[7] offering advice and support in navigating the workplace and decision-making.[6] There is value for employees at all levels, including executives.[5]

Finding mentors outside of the workplace can address individuals' life satisfaction levels, and provide outsider perspectives on work-related issues.[5] Participating in multiple types of mentorship (peer, seniority-based, non-work, etc.) provides more opportunities for an individual's holistic personal development.[5]

Facilitative responses should be used as tools for strengthening relationships, and ensuring individuals feel comfortable self-disclosing. Setting expectations is key in ensuring a successful mentoring relationship.

References

1. Myrick, R. D. (1987). *Developmental guidance and counseling: A practical approach.* Minneapolis, MN: Educational Media Corp.

2. Wittmer, J. & Myrick, R. D. (1980). *Facilitative teaching: Theory and practice.* (2nd ed.). Minneapolis, MN: Educational Media Corp.

3. Cukier, W., Smarz, S. & Yap, M. (2012). Using the diversity audit tool to assess the status of women in the Canadian financial services sector. *The International Journal of Diversity in Organizations, Communities and Nations, 11*(3),15-36.

4. Zachary, L. (2009). Make mentoring work for you: Ten strategies for success. *T + D, 63*(12), 76-77.

5. Zachary, L. & Fischler, L. (2009). Help on the way: Senior leaders can benefit from working with a mentor. *Leadership in Action*, *29*(2), 7-11.

6. Murphy, W. M. & Kram, K. (2010) Understanding non-work relationships in developmental networks. *Career Development International*, *15*(7), 637-663.

7. Zachary, L. (2010). Informal mentoring. *Leadership Excellence*, *27*(2), 16.

8. Clutterbuck, D. (2012). Understanding diversity mentoring. In Clutterback, D., Poulsen, K. M., & Kochan, F. (Eds.), *Developing successful diversity mentoring programmes: An international casebook* (pp. 1-17). New York: McGraw-Hill Education.

9. Kram, K. E. (1985). *Mentoring at work: Developmental relationships in organizational life.* Glenview, IL: Scott, Foresman.

10. Bozeman, B. & Feeney, M. K. (2007). Toward a useful theory of mentoring: A conceptual analysis and critique. *Administration & Society*, *39*(6), 719–739.

Recommended Readings

1. Bachkirova, T., Jackson, P., & Clutterbuck, D. (Eds.). (2011). *Coaching and mentoring supervision: Theory and practice*. New York: McGraw-Hill Education.

2. Clutterback, D., Poulsen, K. M., & Kochan, F. (Eds.). (2012). *Developing successful diversity mentoring programmes: An international casebook*. New York: McGraw-Hill Education.

3. Clutterbuck, D. (2012). Coaching and mentoring in support of management development 1. In Armstrong, S., & Fukami, C. (Eds.), *The SAGE Handbook of Management Learning, Education and Development* (pp.477-497). Thousand Oaks, CA: SAGE.

The 360 Degrees of Mentoring

Ms. Cheryl Kristiansen, P.Eng.
Managing Director, Mitchell Odyssey Foundation
Project Manager, Make Possible Mentoring Network

I have benefited from and been inspired by mentoring opportunities throughout my career – starting in school and continuing today – Mentoring Works! As a female engineer in the male dominated oil and gas sector, most of my mentoring relationships were with male peers. I sought out industry members with complementary skill sets to create mutual learning opportunities and deliver more effective team results. As a management consultant, I continue to create mentoring connections with people all around me – to help develop specific skills, share expertise and advance collaboration opportunities. Mentoring connections have also facilitated volunteer development opportunities including coaching sports – by seeking out role models to fine-tune skills.

Mentoring Works provides an overview of key skills needed to create effective mentoring relationships throughout your career. It is aligned with SCWIST's goal to empower women in STEM through the Make Possible Mentoring Network – which is based on the concept of skills exchange and 360 degree mentoring to advance leadership capacity.

The 360 degrees of mentoring is interactive and continuous – reaching out to people all around you – to create mentoring connections and share skills. It also incorporates the idea of "paying it forward" - people who have benefited from mentors, want to mentor others and share their experiences. Everyone has unique skills, innovative ideas and diverse perspectives to share.

Mentoring – in all its forms - should be a journey of mutual discovery, growth and opportunity. It is a two-way educational process and the learning is connected, collaborative and continuous. Effective mentoring becomes more about learning what you can create together, not just what you can teach the other person. There are many benefits to having several mentors throughout your career – to meet various needs of specific skill development (technical and soft skills); career exploration; leadership development; and sponsorship opportunities. Develop a "mentoring board of directors" and use the Mentoring Works tools to build facilitative conditions and create effective mentoring connections. Mentoring can also explore gender diversity challenges and how to overcome them.

As project manager for SCWIST, I lead the new Make Possible Mentoring Network that encourages women to connect, collaborate and lead through a dedicated mentoring network in STEM. In Make Possible, it's easy to find a mentor, be a mentor, target skills to develop, share expertise, explore career options, find role models and advance leadership opportunities. I encourage all women in STEM to join the free service and build their own 360 Degrees of Mentoring.

www.makepossible.ca

On Engineering

Most of the helping professions are highly visible in our daily lives. When you are sick, you see a doctor, nurse, or pharmacist. When you are in trouble, you call emergency services. When you are ready to learn, you attend class with a teacher, educational assistant, or professor. Engineers improve the lives of everyone around them, but you don't necessarily see them. Instead, you can see the products of their labour: safe roads, buildings and bridges; vehicles, computers, and technology; and the mining, materials, and manufacturing required to create them. Engineers save thousands of lives every day, designing surgical robots, bringing clean water to communities, and developing the clean energy technology we need for the future. Engineers use tools like design processes, safety standards, calculations, and interdisciplinary collaborations, but the core of engineering is simply this: engineers help people solve problems.

What is Engineering?

What is Engineering?
Applying science in everyday life.

environmental protection policies | construction management | advanced composite materials | process improvements | biomedical device design | human-robot interaction | water and sanitation | workplace safety | food supply improvements | technology development | green buildings | lean manufacturing | primary resource industry | communications networks | chemical process scaling for efficiency | machine learning | renewable energy | research and innovation

ENGINEERING:

a [creative engaging rewarding] profession where people [solve problems design solutions help local & global communities and love what they do]

With a Bachelor's Degree in Engineering...

Graduates are **industry-ready** & **hireable**.

Median entry-level salary in B.C.: **$57,141**[1]

Median engineering base salary in B.C.: **$87,000**[1]

95,000+ jobs will be available by the end of 2020 due to retiring engineers.[2]

What skills do I need?

Adaptability

Problem-solving

Attention to detail

Leadership

Curiosity

Communication

Creativity

Teamwork

Working Climate

Engineers work in...

urban centres,   rural communities,   & around the world.

They can work in the field, in the office, or both.

 The Washington Accord allows mobility for P.Engs among 10 countries.

Learn more

www.engineeryourlife.org/

www.egfi-k12.org/

www.apeg.bc.ca/For-Students/High-School-Students

wwest.ca

engcite.ca

Next Steps to Becoming an Engineer...

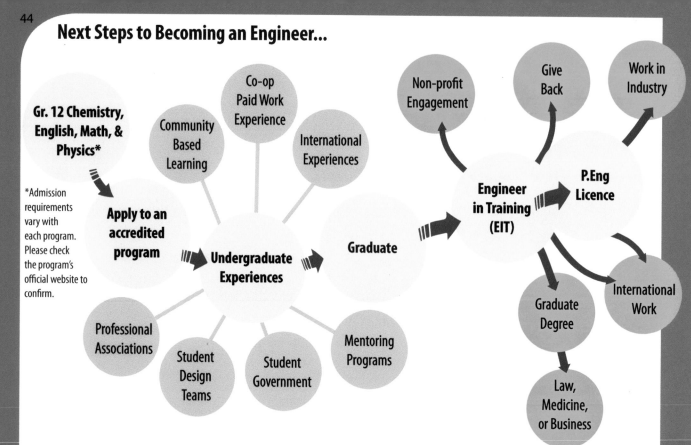

Gr. 12 Chemistry, English, Math, & Physics*

*Admission requirements vary with each program. Please check the program's official website to confirm.

Apply to an accredited program

Community Based Learning

Co-op Paid Work Experience

International Experiences

Undergraduate Experiences

Professional Associations

Student Design Teams

Student Government

Mentoring Programs

Graduate

Non-profit Engagement

Engineer in Training (EIT)

Give Back

Work in Industry

P.Eng Licence

Graduate Degree

International Work

Law, Medicine, or Business

Check out these videos from WISEatlantic to learn more about engineering careers:

http://youtu.be/ JqBLHsNAhBI

http://youtu.be/ dGPP5rHn8ko

http://youtu.be/ Za1JOqYBF-Q

http://youtu.be/ oW2xTH-Z4mE

More videos available at:
www.WISEatlantic.ca/Videos.asp

This Could Be You

AJung Moon

Photo by: Martin Dee, UBC

"I design nonverbal communication cues like hand gestures and gaze for robots so that they can collaborate with people better."

"Working in oil and gas - one of Canada's largest economies - leads to a lot of amazing opportunities."

Kristy Meents

Belinda Li

"Engineering has helped me think creatively to work on solving complex global problems, like making sure people have reliable and sustainable access to safe drinking water."

"As a Building Envelope Engineer, every day we are challenged to investigate and solve existing issues in buildings and design and construct better performing and longer lasting buildings."

Hillary Kernahan

References

1. Association of Professional Engineers and Geoscientists of BC. (2012). Report on members' compensation and benefits. Retrieved from https://www.apeg.bc.ca/Careers/Compensation-Survey
2. Engineers Canada. (2012). The engineering labour market in Canada: Projections to 2020. Retrieved from http://www.engineerscanada.ca/labour-market-report

What Makes a Good Engineer?

Dr. Lesley Shannon, P.Eng.
NSERC Chair for Women in Science and Engineering, BC/Yukon, 2015-2020
Associate Professor, School of Engineering Science, Simon Fraser University

What is engineering? It sounds like a simple question, and yet most people have a hard time answering it. In our everyday lives, we interact with many people with very different "visible" careers- doctors, lawyers, teachers, police officers. Conversely, because of the nature of engineering, even when we encounter engineers, it is often unknowingly.

The word engineer comes from the Latin word "ingeniare" meaning "to contrive, devise" which provides great insight as to the true nature of engineering. In the simplest terms, engineers are problem-solvers. More specifically, engineers apply scientific principles to invent/design/build/ create solutions to problems, while ensuring that these solutions are acceptable both ethically and economically, while respecting the laws and culture of a society. Some examples of the fields of engineering include: Biomedical, Chemical, Computer, Electrical, Environmental, Industrial, and Mechanical. Different engineering fields rely more strongly on different areas of science, depending on their focus. For example, chemical engineering has much closer ties to chemistry, whereas biomedical engineering has closer ties to biology and kinesiology.

Similar to medicine, engineering is a federally self-regulated profession. As such, engineers have a responsibility to the welfare of society at large in everything that they do. Understanding these requirements makes it easier to understand what characteristics are required of an engineer.

To solve problems, engineers must obviously be creative. They must also be adaptable as every problem is a new and unique situation. Since our world is ever-changing, engineers need to be curious, always interested in learning the "why" and "how" of new things. Often engineers have leadership roles, managing a project and a team, and even when they are not working as the team leader, they are generally part of a team. This requires interpersonal capabilities as well as dependability. To solve a problem in a timely and economically viable fashion, engineers need to be organized, pay attention to detail and have a clear sense of time management to ensure that their final solution meets all of the problem's requirements. Engineers also need strong communication skills; they need to be able to communicate ideas and information to teammates and customers, who may or may not have a technical background. Finally, engineers need to be persistent; interesting problems are often challenging and identifying a workable solution may require dedication and perseverance.

As engineers are trained to be adaptable problem solvers, people with engineering degrees often follow extremely varied paths. They create new technology, become lawyers and doctors, manage projects, run companies, and work with people in every walk of life. They work both in cities and rural areas and are able to apply their expertise all over the world. With a desire to change things for the better, engineers are passionate about their work and what they are aiming to achieve. In the future, we need to do a better job informing the public what engineering *really* is to inspire the next generation to pursue this creative and rewarding profession that aims to solve problems and improve society.

For Parents and Guardians

There was a poster in math classrooms across BC some years ago: "Dropping math? Say goodbye to these careers." Though the black and neon of that poster is now dated, the sentiment remains. Science, technology, engineering and mathematics (STEM) form the core of many careers, and are necessary for many more. As your children, and any other young people in your life, begin to make decisions about their educational paths, encourage them to keep their options open. Keeping STEM courses in their curriculum enables them to continue to make choices and decisions as they learn more about potential careers – including careers that we cannot even imagine yet.

Why STEM?
for Parents & Guardians

Science, technology, engineering, and mathematics (STEM) fields often are associated with the stereotype of being "hard," "boring," or "not for me."

Contrary to these stereotypes, careers in STEM fields involve teamwork, creativity, and communication.[1] They often go beyond the laboratory to address current issues our society faces. STEM teams require a variety of people with different skills in order to be successful.

For example, engineering is a creative, engaging, rewarding profession where people solve problems, design solutions, and help local, and global communities. It also requires students to take science and math courses in high school before starting a post-secondary program.

While the young people in your life are starting to make decisions about their future, encourage them to keep STEM options open. Finding role models that help demonstrate what STEM careers involve, and going to events that allow them to try out STEM activities (camps, workshops, open houses) challenge the dominant stereotypes, and are crucial to helping youth make informed career decisions.

3 Reasons to Consider Careers in STEM

The variety of career paths

environmental protection policies | development | advanced composite biomedical device design | textile human-robot interaction | water food supply improvements | buildings | lean manufacturing

construction management | video game materials | process improvements design | transportation networks and sanitation | workplace safety technology development | green | special effects | primary resource

from technicians to Ph.D.s

STEM qualifications are in demand

Contribute to solving today's challenges[4]

Clean water access

Health Informatics

Cyber security

Affordable renewable energy

Improving medicine

Restoring & improving infrastructure

STEM organizations need new workers:

95,000+ engineering jobs available by 2020 due to retiring employees.[2]

100,000+ environmental sector job vacancies in the next decade.[3]

Why should your child keep STEM options open?

70% of top jobs require STEM education[3]

70%

But less than 50% of Canadian high school graduates complete Gr. 11 & 12 math and science[5]

Graduates with STEM degrees:

✓ Earn 26% more on average[3]

✓ Have better job security[3]

✓ Earn more than non-STEM graduates, regardless of career[3]

Unexpected Careers that have STEM Prerequisites[3]

Computer Technology

Chemistry

Physics

Banking management
Welding | Journalism
Broadcasting services management
Industrial design | Crime scene investigation
Animation | Early childhood education | Business administration | Weather forecasting | Chef/Baker | Fitness/Health | Transportation management | Data security analyst
Agriculture/Agribusiness | Carpentry
Dietitian/Nutritionist | Architecture
Forestry | Psychology

Mathematics

Biology

You are influential[6]

76%

of students say their **parents** have the greatest influence on their educational direction.[7]

(teachers are second at 24%)[7]

| Pressure to succeed | → | Supporting a narrow range of careers | → |

Restricts your child's ability to explore alternative careers.[8]

only

28%

of parents talk to their children about the value of optional STEM courses.[9]

STEM Self-Efficacy

Self-Efficacy

a person's belief in their ability to perform a task[10]

strongly predicts[11-13]

academic interest*

persistence in a discipline*

performance*

*in STEM disciplines[12-18]

4 Factors Affect Self-Efficacy[10,19,20]

Social Persuasion	Feedback, support and judgment from others (especially influential figures - parents, teachers).
Mastery Experiences	Has done the task before. Had a chance to learn & practice strategies to do task effectively.
Physiological Factors	How a person interprets their emotional/physiological state. E.g. "butterflies", nerves.
Vicarious Experiences	Learning by observing others doing the task. Role models are important for this.

Self-efficacy influences **the choices we make** in terms of:[21]

- what **goals** we choose
- how much **effort** we put into pursuing them
- our **persistence** when difficulties arise.

The most **influential source** of **STEM self-efficacy**:[22]

Boys ———— **Mastery Experiences**

Girls ⟨ **Social Persuasion**
Vicarious Experiences

Middle school girls' science self-efficacy is **lower than boys'**, & they are **more anxious** about science performance despite achieving higher grades overall.[23]

Perceptions of STEM Professions

Middle school students were asked to **draw** an **engineer**...

... most drew men in "workers'" clothes, seeing engineers as builders or car makers.[24,25]

Students were asked to **draw** a **scientist**...

... most drew men in lab coats.[26,27]

4th year student teachers' drawings of scientists were **more stereotypical** than **Gr. 5 students'.**[27]

only **4%** of Grs. 7 and 9 students think engineering is a profession that can make the world a **better place**.[28]

IN REALITY

Top 10 Employability Skills
for UK STEM Companies:[29]

Communication & interpersonal skills
Problem solving skills
Initiative & self motivation
Working under pressure & to deadlines
Organizational skills
Teamwork
Ability to learn & adapt
Numeracy
Valuing diversity & difference
Negotiation skills

STEM Careers are not Their Stereotypes

Help change the message.

Mentoring Programs

Does this align with my interests?

Learn more about what a job involves

Do I enjoy this work?

Technical College

Undergraduate Degree

Internship/ Volunteer Work

More likely to consider the career as a viable option

Site Visits

Information & experiences inform your child's decisions

Can lead to more interest in the career...

Is this industry a good fit?

Informational Interviews

Open Houses

... and more interest in related courses

What Can We Do?

Encourage your child to pursue a broad range of activities and interests.

Help your child build self-efficacy, not just self-confidence. Give them opportunities outside of class to try new things, and work on mastery.

Be a role model to your child. Try new things. Talk about STEM at home. Consider family outings to STEM destinations, pursuing hands-on activities and do-it-yourself projects at home, and discussing STEM topics on TV or the news.

Expose your child to STEM careers through role models, mentors, workplace visits, the media, summer camps, and career days.

When you see stereotypes in person or in the media, challenge them. Discuss stereotypes with your child. Emphasize that each of us is unique, and have different strengths. Stereotypes do not define us.

If your child appears to be opting out of STEM, encourage them to keep their options open. People with STEM backgrounds are very successful in other fields, but it can be hard to move into STEM if you have opted out of math and science in school.

Overall, take the time to learn about what real STEM careers involve, and provide opportunities for your child to try them out.

References

1. National Academy of Engineering: Committee on Public Understanding of Engineering Messages. (2008). *Changing the conversation: Methods for improving public understanding of engineering.* Washington, D.C., National Academies Press.

2. Engineers Canada. (2012). *The engineering labour market in Canada: Projections to 2020.* Retrieved from http://www.engineerscanada.ca/labour-market-report

3. Let's Talk Science and Amgen Canada. (2013). *Spotlight on science learning: The high cost of dropping science and math.* Retrieved from http://www.letstalkscience.ca/research-publications/publications-by-year.html

4. National Academy of Engineering (2008). *Grand challenges for engineering.* Retrieved from http://www.engineeringchallenges.org

5. Let's Talk Science and Amgen Canada. (2012). *Spotlight on science learning: A benchmark of Canadian talent.* Retrieved from http://www.letstalkscience.ca/research-publications/publications-by-year.html

6. Bardick, A.D., Bernes, K.B., Magnusson, K.D. (2004). Junior high career planning: What students want. *Canadian Journal of Counselling, 38*(2), 104-117.

7. Let's Talk Science and Amgen Canada. (2014). *Spotlight on science learning: Shaping tomorrow's workforce - what do Canada's teens think about their future?* Retrieved from http://www.letstalkscience.ca/research-publications/publications-by-year.html

8. Middleton, E.B., & Loughead, T.A. (1993). Parental influence on career development: An integrative framework for adolescent career counselling. *Journal of Career Development, 19*(3), 161-173.

9. Let's Talk Science and Amgen Canada. (2015). *Spotlight on science learning: Exploring parental influence.* Retrieved from http://www.letstalkscience.ca/research-publications/publications-by-year.html

10. Bandura, A. (1977). Self-efficacy: Toward a unifying theory of behavioural change. *Psychological Review, 84*(2), 191-215.

11. Lent, R.W., Brown, S.D., & Hackett, G. (2000). Contextual supports and barriers to career choice: A social cognitive analysis. *Journal of Counseling Psychology, 47*, 36-49.

12. Lent, R.W., Brown, S.D., & Larkin, K.C. (1984). Relation of self-efficacy expectations to academic achievement and persistence. *Journal of Counseling Psychology, 31*, 356-362.

13. Lent, R.W., Sheu, H-B., Singly, D., Schimdt, J.A., Schmidt, L.C., & Gloster, C.S. (2008). Longitudinal relations of self-efficacy to outcome expectations, interests, and major choice goals in engineering students. *Journal of Vocational Behaviour, 73*, 328-335.

14. Betz, N.E., & Hackett., G. (1983). The relationship of mathematics self-efficacy expectations to the selection of science-based college majors. *Journal of Vocational Behaviour, 23*, 329-345.

15. Fouad, N.A., & Smith, P.L. (1996). A test of social cognitive model for middle school students: Math and science. *Journal of Counselling Psychology, 43*, 338-346.

16. Lapan, R.T., Boggs, K.R., & Morrill, W.J. (1996). Efficacy expectations and vocational interests as mediators between sex and choice of math/science college majors: A longitudinal study. *Journal of Vocational Behaviour, 49,* 277-291.

17. Luzzo, D.A., Hasper, P., Albert, K.A., Bibby, M.A., & Martinelli, E.A. (1999). Effects of self-efficacy-enhancing interventions on the math/science self-efficacy and career interests, goals, and actions of career undecided college students. *Journal of Counseling Psychology, 46*, 233-243.

18. Schaefers, K.G., Epperson, D.L., & Natura, M.M. (1997). Women's career development: Can theoretically derived variables predict persistence in engineering majors? *Journal of Counselling Psychology, 49,* 173-183.

19. Gist, M. E., & Mitchell, T. R. (1992). Self-efficacy: A theoretical analysis of its determinants and malleability. *Academy of Management Review, 17,* 183–211.

20. Pajares, F. (2005). Gender differences in mathematics self-efficacy beliefs. In A. M. Gallagher & J. C. Kaufman (Eds.), *Gender differences in mathematics: An integrative psychological approach* (pp. 294–315). New York: Cambridge University Press.

21. Bandura, A. (1997). *Self-efficacy: The exercise of control.* New York: W. H. Freeman and Company.

22. Zeldin, A. L., & Pajares, F. (2000). Against the odds: Self-efficacy beliefs of women in mathematical, scientific, and technological careers. *American Educational Research Journal, 37*, 215–246.

23. Britner, S. L., & Pajares, F. (2006). Sources of science self-efficacy beliefs of middle school students. *Journal of Research in Science Teaching, 43*, 485–499.

24. Fralick, B., Kearn, J., Thompson, S., & Lyons, J. (2009). How middle schoolers draw engineers and scientists. *Journal of Science Education Technology, 18*, 60-73.

25. Karatas, F.O., Micklos, A., & Bodner, G.M. (2011). Sixth-grade students' views of the nature of engineering and images of engineers. *Journal of Science Education Technology, 20*, 123-125.

26. Ruiz-Mallén, I., & Escalas, M.T. (2012). Scientists seen by children: A case study in Catalonia, Spain. *Science Communication, 34*(4), 520-545.

27. Unver, A.O. (2010). Perceptions of scientists: A comparative study of fifth graders and fourth year student teachers. *Necatibey Faculty of Education Electronic Journal of Science and Mathematics Education, 4*(1), 11-28.

28. Franz-Odendaal, T., Blotnicky, K., French, F., & Joy, P. (2014). *Career choices and influencers in science, technology, engineering and math: An analysis of the maritime provinces.* Retrieved from http://www.wiseatlantic.ca/Researchteam.asp

29. STEMNET (n.d). *Top 10 employability skills.* Retrieved from http://www.exeter.ac.uk/ambassadors/HESTEM/resources/General/STEMNET%20Employability%20skills%20guide.pdf

Recommended Reading

1. Subject choice in STEM: Factors influencing young people in education. http://www.wellcome.ac.uk/stellent/groups/corporatesite/@msh_publishing_group/documents/web_document/wtx063082.pdf

2. http://www.wherestemcantakeyou.co.uk/docs/Why_STEM_Careers.pdf

Perspective References

1. Let's Talk Science. (2014). *Spotlight on science learning: Shaping tomorrow's workforce – what do Canada's teens think about their futures?* Retrieved from http://www.letstalkscience.ca/research-publications/spotlight-on-science-learning.html

2. Smith, S.L., Choueiti, M., & Pieper, K. (2015). *Gender bias without borders: An investigation of female characters in popular films across 11 countries.* Retrieved from the Geena Davis Institute on Gender in Media website: http://seejane.org/symposiums-on-gender-in-media/gender-bias-without-borders/

From One Parent to Another
Supporting Daughters to Consider STEM Careers

Dr. Sheryl Staub-French, P.Eng
Goldcorp Professor for Women in Engineering | Director, eng•cite
Associate Professor, UBC Department of Civil Engineering

What I have learned in my own path to engineering, in conversations with other parents, and as a parent myself, is the importance of intention. Parents have the greatest influence on their children's educational direction.[1] So we must be very intentional of the messages we want to send our children about what is possible for them, what they are capable of, and what skills are needed to navigate it all. We must also be very intentional in understanding our own biases (see the chapter on implicit bias) and our own perceptions about engineering and who can become an engineer (see the chapter on 'What is engineering?').

At a basic level, we want girls to know from an early age that they are equally capable in math and science, that engineering is a possible career path that is available to them, and that engineering can provide a rewarding, creative and meaningful profession for them if they choose it. But we must be intentional about how we convey that message because they are also being bombarded with other messages about how they should look, how they should behave, and what is possible for them.

"If she can see it, she can be it."[2] This is a message I have taken to heart as a parent and educator. For me, this shows up in three distinct ways. First, we must be deliberate about exposing girls to role models. I have done this by introducing my daughter to different professional women, including astronauts, politicians, scientists, business leaders, and of course, engineers. Sometimes these introductions have been in person, but most of the time I have done this through articles and videos I have found online. And we must remember that we are role models and our children's teachers are role models too (so parents and teachers, no saying *"I'm not good at math"*).

Second, we must be aware of the role models they are being exposed to in the media. Unfortunately, female characters in the media are still being portrayed in stereotyped ways and with an overemphasis on their physical appearance.[2] As a parent, I have tried to find programming with strong female lead characters but this is something I still struggle with since there aren't as many options. What I have done though, is point out all the inappropriate or inaccurate messages they are receiving. I am starting to think that I may be doing this too often though since my children now exclaim *"we know mom, girls don't really look that way!"* Third, we must be mindful of the messages we send girls with the toys we buy for them. As a parent, I have been shocked by how many toys have become gendered. Even Lego, my favorite toy as a child, has made building things a gendered activity. When I was growing up, Lego blocks were green, blue, red and yellow. Now, they have purple and pink Lego blocks for girls with the primary themes centred on 'friends', not building stuff. So now my favorite toy is Keva blocks, since they are gender neutral and equally awesome at building (see the awesome tower my daughter built!).

Even though I am a professor of engineering, I still have to work at this. But I think being aware of the different messages that our children are receiving and being intentional about the messages we give them, will go a long way in shaping their perceptions of what is possible. And for our girls (and boys), we want them to believe that anything is possible!

To Summarize:

You've seen the data, and now you need the elevator pitch for the senior leadership at your organization. Why do all of these behaviours and assumptions matter? Why should anyone care?

This is our pitch: a single page to make people pause, consider, and ask for more.

Executive Summary

Why does it matter?

The business case is clear. Among other benefits, gender diversity can:

- Increase financial performance;
- Provide access to more talent;
- Strengthen innovation;
- Improve governance.

Having a critical mass of 30% or at least 2 or 3 women on a board **decreases groupthink**[6]

Gender diversity has a positive effect on **team innovation** in radical research[2]

Return on Invested Capital[1]

+26% ↑   9.1% Top Quartile
7.2% Bottom Quartile

Fortune 500 companies with the most and least women Board Directors; 2004-2008

Also: +16% Return on Sales[1]

Women directors:

improve a firm's ability to navigate complex strategic issues[3]

positively influence board strategic direction & tasks[4,5]

Priorities

On Microaggressions

Sometimes unconscious, microaggressions are subtle, mundane exchanges that communicate hostile, derogatory, or negative messages to individuals based on group membership.[11,12]

Microinsults, microinvalidations, and microassaults perpetuate stereotype threat[7,8] and create a hostile work environment[9,10].

"A person catcalls you."   "That's so gay."
"Why do you have to be so loud?"
"You're a *@^!#&."
"People stare when you hold your partner's hand."
"A person walks past you, and clutches their purse."
"You speak English very well."
"You must be good at math."   "Where are you from?"

First Steps: Communication

What do you communicate about your company? How do you represent science, technology, engineering and math (STEM) careers? Do you:

- Use gender-inclusive language?
- Use photos that show both men and women in technical roles?
- Talk about your corporate values?
- Tell people that you value diversity?

Check: websites, reports, staff meetings and communications, shareholder meetings, etc. Are you communicating, explicitly and implicitly, that your company is a great place for both men and women in STEM?

First Steps: People-Friendly Policies

It isn't about women-friendly policies - it is about people-friendly policies.
Create a welcoming workplace that respects employees' lives outside the office:

- Offer flexible working arrangements;
- Encourage parental and adoptive leave for both men and women;
- Provide benefits that work for people in a wide range of situations;
- Provide professional development.

Check: do your policies match your practices? A policy that staff feel they cannot use is worse than no policy at all.

On Implicit Bias

Unconscious bias refers to the assumptions and conclusions we jump to without thinking.[14] Everyone has unconscious biases. Being aware of these biases is the first step to combating them.

Women are **50%** more likely to advance in an orchestra audition if they **can't be seen**.[13]

Be a Leader

Everyone has a role to play in increasing gender diversity in STEM. No matter what your position is, there are three simple things you can do to be a leader:

1. Be aware of your own biases. Take the Harvard implicit bias tests at www.implicit.harvard.edu.
2. Be aware of how you represent STEM and your organization, personally and at work.
3. Advocate for and implement people-friendly policies.

   If you would like to learn more about gender diversity, visit wwest.mech.ubc.ca/diversity

On Stereotype Threat

Stereotype threat refers to the concern with being viewed through the lens of a stereotype.[17] It is caused by cues in the situation that remind people of negative stereotypes.[15,16]

Anxiety over confirming these stereotypes can impair an individual's ability to perform up to their full potential.[18]

References

For: Why Does it Matter?

1. Catalyst (2011). The bottom line: Corporate performance and women's representation on boards (2004–2008). Retrieved from http://www.catalyst.org/knowledge/bottom-line-corporate-performance-and-womens-representation-boards-20042008
2. Diaz-Garcia, C., Gonzalez-Moreno, A., & Saez-Martinez, F.J. (2013). Gender diversity within R&D teams: Its impact on radicalness of innovation. Innovation: Management, Policy, & Practice, 15(2), 149- 160.
3. Francoeur, C., Labelle, R., & Sinclair-Desgagné, B. (2008). Gender diversity in corporate governance and top management. Journal of Business Ethics, 81(1), 83-95.
4. Lückerath-Rovers, M. (2013). Women on boards and firm performance. Journal of Management & Governance, 17(2), 491-509.
5. Nielsen, S., & Huse, M. (2010). The contribution of women on boards of directors: Going beyond the surface. Corporate Governance: An International Review, 18(2), 136-148.
6. Torchia, M., Calabrò, A., & Huse, M. (2011). Women directors on corporate boards: From tokenism to critical mass. Journal of Business Ethics, 102(2), 299–317.

For: On Microaggressions

7. Cadinu, M., Maass, A., Rosabianca, A., & Kiesner, J. (2005). Why do women underperform under stereotype threat? Evidence for the role of negative thinking. Psychological Science, 16, 572 – 578.
8. Steele, C. M., Spencer, S. J., & Aronson, J. (2002). Contending with group image: The psychology of stereotype and social identity threat. In M. Zanna (Ed.), Advances in experimental social psychology (Vol. 23, pp. 379 – 440). New York: Academic Press.
9. Rowe, M. P. (1990). Barriers to equality: The power of subtle discrimination to maintain unequal opportunity. Employee Responsibilities and Rights Journal, 3, 153 – 163.
10. Solórzano, D., Ceja, M., & Yosso, T. (2000). Critical race theory, racial microaggressions, and campus racial climate: The experiences of African American college students. The Journal of Negro Education, 69(1/2) , 60 – 73.
11. Sue, D. W., Capodilupo, C. M., Torino, G. C., Bucceri, J. M., Holder, A. M. B., Nadal, K. L., & Esquilin,M. (2007). Racial microaggressions in everyday life: Implications for clinical practice. American Psychologist, 62, 271-286.
12. Sue, D.W. (2010). Microaggressions in everyday life: Race, gender, and sexual orientation. Hoboken, NJ: John Wiley & Sons.

For: On Implicit Bias

13. Goldin, C. & Rouse, C. (2000). Orchestrating impartiality: The impact of "blind" auditions on female musicians. The American Economic Review, 90(4), 715-741.
14. Network Exchange. (2012). Unconscious bias. Retrieved from http://online.fliphtml5.com/hcxu/wfbe/#p=6

For: On Stereotype Threat

15. Bell, A. E., Spencer, S. J., Iserman, E., & Logel, C. R. (2003). Stereotype threat and women's performance in engineering. Journal of Engineering Education, 92(4), 307-312.
16. Nguyen, H.-H. D., & Ryan, A. M. (2008). Does stereotype threat affect test performance of minorities and women? A meta-analysis of experimental evidence. Journal of Applied Psychology, 93, 1314-1334.
17. Steele, C.M., & Aronson, J. (1995). Stereotype threat and the intellectual test performance of African-Americans. Journal of Personality and Social Psychology, 69, 797-811.
18. Walton, G., & Spencer, S. (2009). Latent ability: Grades and test scores systematically underestimate the intellectual ability of negatively stereotyped students. Psychological Science, 20(9), 1132-1139

Recommended Readings

For more information on these topics, please consider reading the rest of this series at wwest.mech.ubc.ca/diversity.

Beyond Gender: Fostering Inclusivity in Engineering

Mr. Kim Allen, FEC, FCEA, P.Eng., MBA
CEO, Engineers Canada

The engineering profession has come a long way in fostering diversity, and while it continues to evolve there is still much distance to cover. In 1978, women comprised a mere one percent of Canada's engineers.[1] In 36 years, this has grown from 1,500 to over 32,000, representing 12 per cent of the engineering profession. This occurred because of the hard work of many sector players. However, more work needs to be done to realize the true gender diversity that is necessary.

The business case for gender diversity has been clear for decades. Diversity in a workforce provides significant advantages in economic performance, better business capacity, less turnover, and increased creativity. Decisions made with varied points of view and that bring together different life experiences, perspectives, values, communication, management, and leadership styles are more effective and better reflect economic and business realities. Even while recognizing the need and benefit, increasing gender diversity in the engineering profession continues to be a challenge.

The culture of historically male-dominated professions like engineering developed in an era that no longer reflects the needs, expectations, or composition of today's labour force. The engineering profession is aware of the necessity for change, and this is reflected in the national adoption of Engineers Canada's 30 by 30 goal by all engineering regulators and several post-secondary institutions.

Numeric goals are important, particularly because they create a critical mass that turns transformation into a new societal norm; however, numbers are meaningless if they are not supported by a strategy to change the culture of a profession which still erects individual, organizational, and societal barriers. This culture shift is integral in combating the false assumption that a quota leads to inclusion and advancement based on gender rather than the merit of an individual. Indeed, quotas can create an effect opposite to their goal – instead of reducing or eliminating gender discrimination, they can foster resistance to the change. Preventing this requires focussing on engaging, including, and embracing gender diversity as means to improving the profession.

Diversity does not start and end with gender. As Canadian demographics change, diversity also means embracing the multinational, multigenerational, gender-diverse makeup of the country and ensuring this is reflected at a professional level in a way that looks beyond gender ratios and toward promoting a culture of inclusivity.

Across the industrialized world, the upcoming retirement of baby boomers will mean that professions like engineering are going to lose a large number of skilled, senior-level employees in a short period of time. A strong and technically skilled engineering profession is a key component of a successful twenty-first-century economy. Strengthening diversity will address national skilled labour needs and better insulate the profession from these strong demographic effects.

The engineering profession's key stakeholders - schools, universities, professional bodies and industries will need to work together to create a diversity management plan that goes beyond reaching a target for the number of women in the profession, and that reaches true gender diversity and inclusivity in the profession.

1. Individuals registered with an engineering regulator

Reusing These Materials

This book is meant to be shared. Please make sure you do so in a way that reflects the work that has gone into it.

If you want to photocopy a page, we recommend printing the online versions of each chapter. These can be found at wwest.mech.ubc.ca/diversity/

The illustrations and layout of this book are original; please do not copy or reproduce this without permission from the authors.

The authors of the Perspective chapters retain their copyright, and their work may not be reproduced without permission.

To cite information in this book, please adhere to the following suggestions. The following are listed in APA format; please follow the guidelines of the citation style you are using.

Recommended citation for infographic chapter:
Parker, R., Pelletier, J., & Croft, E. (2015). *WWEST's gender diversity in STEM: A briefing on women in science and engineering.* San Francisco, CA: Blurb.

Recommended citation for a Perspective Chapter (example):
Schmader, T. (2015). Reducing stereotype threat. In R. Parker, J. Pelletier, & E. Croft (Eds.), *WWEST's gender diversity in STEM: A briefing on women in science and engineering.* (pp. 17). San Francisco, CA: Blurb.

About WWEST

Westcoast Women in Engineering, Science & Technology, commonly referred to as WWEST, is the operating name for the programs of the National Sciences and Engineering Research Council of Canada (NSERC) Chair for Women in Science and Engineering for the British Columbia and Yukon Region.

WWEST opens doors and invites girls, women, and everyone else to engage with STEM: science, technology, engineering and math. Through policy advocacy, research, and grassroots outreach, WWEST aims to attract and retain women in STEM careers.

Our Mission:

The mission of the Chair is to advance engineering and science as welcoming careers that serve our world through holistic understanding and creative, appropriate and sustainable solutions.

Our Goals:

The primary focus of the NSERC Chair for Women in Science and Engineering (BC/Yukon) is to promote Science and Engineering as an excellent career choice for women and other under-represented groups, and to identify and eliminate barriers that result in attrition from these career paths. To address the challenges described above, three strategic thrusts for this Chair, aligned with the overarching NSERC goals for this program, are identified:

1. Awareness and Outreach
2. Recruitment
3. Retention and Industry Support

Our History and Our Future:

WWEST was founded by the 2010-2015 NSERC Chair for Women in Science and Engineering for BC and Yukon, Dr. Elizabeth Croft at the University of British Columbia.

The WWEST brand will remain with the NSERC Chair for Women in Science and Engineering for BC and Yukon, under the new 2015-2020 Chairholder, Dr. Lesley Shannon at Simon Fraser University.

About the Authors

Dr. Elizabeth Croft, Ph.D., P.Eng., Fellow Engineers Canada, Fellow American Society of Mechanical Engineers, is a Professor of Mechanical Engineering and Associate Dean, Education and Professional Development for the Faculty of Applied Science and UBC. She held the NSERC Chair for Women in Science and Engineering, BC-Yukon at UBC and led the WWEST program for women in engineering, science and technology. from 2010-2015.

As director of the Collaborative Advanced Robotics and Intelligent Systems (CARIS) Laboratory at UBC, Dr. Croft's research investigates how robotic systems can behave, and be perceived to behave, in a safe, predictable, and helpful manner, and how people interact with and understand robotic systems. Applications of this work range from manufacturing assembly to healthcare and assistive technology. Elizabeth received a Peter Wall Early Career Scholar award in 2001, the Association of Professional Engineers and Geoscientists (BC) Professional Service Award in 2005, the Award for the Support of Women in the Engineering Profession, Canadian Council of Professional Engineers in 2006, an NSERC Accelerator award in 2007, and a YWCA Women of Distinction Award in 2013. She enjoys running and quiet beaches.

Rebekah Parker lives on unceded Coast Salish territories and is an experiential educator with a passion for ecojustice, the outdoors, and bicycles. As the Education and Outreach Coordinator for WWEST from 2013-2015 she engaged hundreds of high school students in hands-on engineering activities, and supported WWEST programming from event logistics to researching and co-developing the Gender Diversity 101 series.

In the summer of 2015 she was the Program Assistant for the Pearson Seminar on Youth Leadership, living in community with, and co-teaching 90 youth from 30+ countries around the world. She has developed curriculum with the Culturally Relevant Urban Wellness (CRUW) program, facilitated social justice workshops with Check Your Head, and currently is a Bicycle Safety Instructor with LIFECycle. When she's not in the city, she's often found bicycle touring around the Salish Sea. She is pursuing a Master's in Ecojustice and Sustainability Education at UBC, and is the Community-Based Experiential Learning Assistant for UBC's Faculty of Applied Science.

Jennifer Pelletier was the Manager for WWEST, the program of Dr. Elizabeth Croft's NSERC Chair for Women in Science and Engineering (BC / Yukon), for the duration of the mandate, 2010-2015. She also held the positions of Program Administrator, for the Engendering Engineering Success Research Project and Network Coordination Administrator, for the National CWSE Network.

She has been recognized with a 2015 UBC Alma Mater Society Just Desserts Award, a UBC Applied Science 2012 Dean's Award for Excellence in Service, and a UBC 2010 President's Staff Award in the category of Enhancing the UBC Experience. She was also named the Honourary President of the Engineering Undergraduate Society for the 2009-2010 school year. Her educational background is in Adult Education and project management.

She is currently the Manager, Technical Administration and Industry Relations for UBC's Department of Mechanical Engineering. Her favourite moments outside of work include road-tripping across the north with a quilting hoop in her lap, and hiking to rock arches, sand dunes, and cliff faces for sunrise photography.

CPSIA information can be obtained at www.ICGtesting.com
Printed in the USA
LVIW01n0327020216
473212LV00007B/8